A Book of Stenography

Published by :
Lotus Press Publishers & Distributors

A Book of Stenography

For the students of CBSE+2, Vocational, Secretarial & Commercial Practice, NOS, ITIs, YMCA, YWCA, Polytechnic, Diploma & Degree Courses

Harvinder Singh

4735/22, Prakash Deep Building
Ansari Road, Darya Ganj,
New Delhi - 110002

Lotus Press : Publishers & Distributors
Unit No. 220, 2nd Floor, 4735/22, Prakash Deep Building,
Ansari Road, Darya Ganj, New Delhi- 110002
Ph.: 41325510, 98118-38000
• E-mail : lotuspress1984@gmail.com
www.lotuspress.co.in

A Book of Stenography

ISBN: 81-8382-023-9

Printed & Published by : **Lotus Press Publishers & Distributors,** New Delhi-02

CONTENTS

- **Form of Verbs**

  Form of Verbs with distinctive outlines for similar forms.

- **Preposition**

  Preposition and its proper use with outlines.

- **Punctuation & Capital Letters**

  Proper use of punctuation marks and Capital Letters with some Un-punctuated / Punctuated passage.

- **Marking of Mistakes**

  How to mark and analyse the mistakes in shorthand passages, Analysis Sheet of Mistakes for day-to-day improvement.

- **Special outlines**

  Definition of phraseography, its proper use, advanced outlines of important & common phrases related to different fields.

****

PREFACE

As a Private Secretary and practitioner, I have always felt that there is always scope for making improvement in teaching stenography in order that the students learn the subject in a systematic manner. I usually cast myself in the position of a learner and try to find out where and when they stumble. I have often seen and observed that the learners loose their interest either in the initial stage of learning and largely during the stage when they fail to pick up speed. This happens mainly owing to the lack of proper guidance. I have attempted this book in such a manner that the learners not only learn the outlines but understand and familiarize themselves with all the facets of the subject of stenography as a subject and also learn and make use of the attendant issues while studying stenography.

This book especially meant for the use of trainees and high speed aspirants who are appearing in competitive examinations conducted by various Selection Boards as also useful to the trainees of ITIs, Commercial & Vocational Institutions, Secretarial Practice etc. The entire matter of this book is co-related with one another to be a perfect stenographer.

I hope that this book will be extremely useful to all the learners at every stage of their course of learning. I am certain if the guiding principles, which enunciated in this book, are followed by the learners, it will help in instilling continuous interest in them. I sure, if this objective is achieved, the drop out rate of learners will be drastically reduced.

The present publication is a collection of many aspects of Stenography - a method of writing rapidly by substituting characters, abbreviations, symbols for letters, words or phrases. The present book would help the readers a long way to get an accurate and fascinating glimpse into this field. It also presents an overview of the main facets and essential ingredients of Stenography. This book is based on my twenty years of practical experience in this trade. No author writes a book without taking enormous help from others. I have also drawn insights and ideas from many sources including magazines, books, and lectures.

Let us not forget that a perfect stenographer have a good knowledge of all the facets of the subject. The book in your hand will help you to achieve this prime objective.

Harvinder Singh

I-172, Karam Pura,
New Delhi-110015
Mob: 9810359632
E.Mail: harvinder_sir@yahoo.co.in

ACKNOWLEDGEMENT

I am grateful to my family members, friends & colleagues who persistently suggested me to write this book. It would be impossible to mention by names all the friends and colleagues who have helped me in their various ways for each interaction of this book.

I also wish to express my gratitude to all those persons who rendered their invaluable assistance by cheerfully under tremendous pressure and contributed their efforts, time, thoughts and advice in writing of this book.

Every effort has been made to give credit where it is due for the material contained herein. If inadvertently we have omitted giving credit, future publications will give due credit to those that are brought to the author's attention.

****

Brief for Beginners

Introduction, Consonants & Vowels, Diphthongs, Triphones, Consonants - R/H, Small and Big Circle for S/Z/Ses/SW, Loop St and STR, Consonant L - Upward, Downward & Halving, Double Consonants - Straights & Curves, Final Hook for N and F/V, Large Final Hook, Abbreviated & Medial W, Compound Consonants, Doubling Principles, Prefixes, Suffixes, Diphones, Intersections and Figures.

INTRODUCTION

The system of vocalized shorthand language was invented and introduced by Sir Isaac Pitman in England in 1837. He described it as **"Phonography"** or **"Writing by sound"**. The characters, signs or symbols of shorthand are called the phonetic alphabet. Shorthand is a systemized method of abbreviation. We can also say that Shorthand is a script with which human thoughts can be recorded sufficiently & effectively and speak out for the benefit of others in a short time as the speed and accuracy are the prime factors of shorthand language.

Shorthand is an **"art"** and is totally different from the other languages. This art is represented by various sounds at all levels with the usage of many signs / indications. These signs, when joined with one another, give pace to writing and helps to record more spoken words with little efforts resulting into accuracy with good speed. The art of stenography means to write a communication in shorthand and then transcribe it in the respective language script. Thus, the art of stenography includes type-writing and shorthand writing. That is why, these are called twin-arts. Shorthand is used to record the proceedings of the Legislative Bodies, hon'ble Courts, Business correspondence etc.

The word **'Graphy'** is derived from **'Graphein'** which means the art of writing. Phonography is the old name of stenography. Shorthand has been variously known as **'teenygraphy'** (quick writing), **'brachygraphy'** (short writing), **zeiglographia; semography; stenography or shorthand** (narrow writing) and hundreds of systems have been experimented and used since immemorial long time.

Pitman's Shorthand entered into towards close of the 19th century during the British period and after its successful use in trade and commerce, it is gradually established in the various fields.

****

PART -I

It is an established fact that if you intend to learn any language, knowledge of consonants and vowels is essential to be learnt at it's preliminary stage to proceed further.

It is known to everyone, who are going to learn shorthand language, that in English language, there are **26** alphabets consisting five vowels - **"a, e, i, o, u"** and **21** consonants. On the other hand, in Shorthand language, there are **24** consonants and **12** vowels of which covers almost all the sounds of all the consonants pronounced with the help of throat or lips. Throat and lips play frequently with each other to make the sound of consonants. According to Indian Linguists **"Consonants are the body of a language and vowels are its soul."**

If the sound of letters comes from the inside of throat, without friction of tongue or lips called Vowels. There are 12 vowels in shorthand language, out of which, six are known as **long or heavy vowels** having long sound, and the remaining six are called **short or light vowels** with light sound.

CONSONANTS

Shorthand is a language which is totally different from the other languages like;

(i) **Light / Dark impression** : To differentiate the meaning, the consonants / strokes are always written by giving light / dark impression for which trainee has to use the Lead Pencil instead of Ball Point Pen. At the stage of higher speed, use of good Ink Pen is recommended for speed which to some extent not possible with the help of pencil. Learner may note that dark strokes are not written in the upward direction.

(ii), **Size of consonants** : The consonants snould be written about one-sixth of an inch long by giving the shape in original, halving, doubling principle in the Shorthand. Keep the size of the strokes/lines equal i.e. 3/4 cms. means strokes must be of a uniform length.

(iii) **Placing of vowels & position of consonants** : It always help one to obtain speed and accuracy without mistakes.

(iv) **Outlines** : Shorthand outlines should always be written only on the Notebook having horizontal lines (ruled paper) instead of drawing copy, to maintain the size, place and position of all the strokes perfect and proper. So, use only shorthand Note Book for practice as it requires the practice of turning of pages unlike other notebook.

Mainly, there are two types of strokes in Shorthand i.e. **(i) Straight Strokes** and **(ii) Shallow Curved Strokes** for which the following geometrical diagrams / forms are used to represent the sounds of consonants (except W, Y and H which are the combination of straight and a curve stroke which are called mixed stroke). In other words, strokes are written in three directions in shorthand e.g. Downward, Horizontal, Upward.

- **Straight Stroke** :
- **Shallow Curve Strokes** :

P (Pee)		B (Bee)		T (Tee)	
D (Dee)		Ch (Chay)		J (Jay)	
K (Kay)		G (Gay)		F (Ef)	
V (Vee)		Th (ith)		Th (thee)	
S (Ess)		Z (Zee)		SH (ish)	
ZH (zhee)		M (Em)		N (En)	
NG (ing)		L (El)		R (Dn)	
R (Up)		W (way)		Y (Yay)	
H (Hay) Dn		H (Hay) Up			

Note: Learners may note that the Consonants should thoroughly be practised regularly at least one page of each consonant attentively by adopting the procedure and method as is given in PART- I to attain good and high speed with accuracy.

PART - II VOWELS

We have already learnt in **PART- I** that in Shorthand language, there are **six long vowels with long sound** and **six short vowels with short sound** which are represented by heavy dot / dash and light dot / dash respectively.

Every stroke has two sides i.e. Left-hand side and Right-hand side. If the vowel or its sound comes before the stroke, it is indicated alongside before the stroke means left side, if the vowel comes after the stroke, it is indicated alongside after the stroke means right side e.g.

Left side

Right side

All the vowels are represented / placed at three places i.e.

Ist Place - from where the stroke / consonant is started.
IInd Place - at the middle of the consonant.
IIIrd Place - at the end of the consonant.

The places of the vowels are taken from the point where the stroke begins.

In Brief: Vowels are put in three positions, i.e.,

	Ist	2nd	3rd	Ist	2nd	3rd
Long	āh	ā	ēē	āw	ō	ōō
Short	ă	ĕ	ĭ	ŏ	ŭ	ŏŏ

Note If the vowel is not placed correctly at the right place, the identity of the word get lost or in other words meaning / sound of word get completely changed. Therefore, learners should adhere to the instructions given at the beginning of the course as well as during the class.

IInd Place vowel of which strokes should be written "On the line"

Sound of Long **"a"** is represented by heavy dot (.)

Aid .... Paid .... Bait .... Date ....

Tape .... Ape ...... Pay ...... Abe ...... Age ......

Babe .... Page .... Fade .... Faith ....

Shape .... Bathe .... Shade .... Say ....

Weigh .... Weighed .... Raid .... Eight ....

Pear .... Share .... Fair .... Bear ....

Take .... Ache .... Gay .... Make ....

Name .... Mail .... Shake .... Change ....

Aim .... May .... Came .... Cake ....

Sound of short **"e"** is represented by light dot (.)

Edd .... Bet .... Debt .... Jet ....

Etch .... Edge .... Pep .... Ted ....

Fed .... Fetch .... Debt .... Essay ....

Death .... Shed .... Led .... Red ....

Egg .... Keg .... Web .... Wedge ....

Check .... Length .... Wet ....

Sound of long **"o"** is represented by heavy dash (-)

Boat .... Show .... Bow .... Vote ....

Toe .... Oat .... Foe .... Oath .... So ....

Owes .... Showed .... Both .... Rote ....

Dome .... Woe .... Door .... Pour ....

Shore .... Four .... Wrote .... Coal ....

Goal .... Load .... Joke .... Comb ....

No .... Know .... Rore .... Fourth ....

- Sound of short "u" is represented by light dash (-)

Up .... Judge .... Dutch .... Touch ....

Us .... Tub .... Rut .... Dumb ....

Gum .... Love .... Thumb .... Lunch ....

Bunch .... Tongue .... Rung .... Munch ....

Leg .... Cup .... Month .... Urge ....

Ist Place vowel of which strokes should be written "Above the line'

- Sound of long **"ah"** is represented by heavy dot (.)

Calm .... Palm .... Balm .... Pa ....

Ma .... Shah .... Arch .... Park ....

- Sound of short **"a"** is represented by light dot (.)

Map .... Away .... Manage .... Annum ....

Package .... At .... Add .... Bank ....

Pal .... Bath .... Attack .... Catch ....

Ashore .... Allay .... Cap ....

Arrow .... Back .... Pack .... Tap ....

Sound of long **"aw"** is represented by heavy dash (-)

Saw .... Bought .... Auto .... Talk ....

Paw .... Pawed .... Tall .... Chalk ....

Jaw .... Law .... Paul .... Thawed ....

- Sound of short "o" is represented by light dash (-)

Top .... Odd .... Shop .... Doll .... Watch ....

Job .... Off .... Shock .... Got ....

Lodge .... Rod .... Rock .... Wrong ....

Polly .... Dolly .... Mocking .... Or ....

IIIrd Place vowel of which strokes should be written "through the line".

Note Learners may note that if the IIIrd Place vowel comes in between two strokes, then the vowel indication is to be placed before the IInd stroke in the IIIrd Place to avoid any confusion while placing the vowel.

Sound of long "e" is represented by heavy dot (.)

Eat .... Feed .... Theme .... Keep ....

Each .... See .... Ease .... Deep ....

Leave .... Teach .... Team .... Deal ....

Meal .... Eel .... Peel .... Keyed ....

Heed .... Key .... Reach .... Relief ....

Relieve .... Ear .... Fear ....

Sound of short "i" is represented by light dot (.)

If .... Bit .... Ship .... Live ....

Pick .... Big .... Inch .... Kid ....

Ill .... Bill .... Mill .... Milk ....

Thick .... Width .... Ring ....

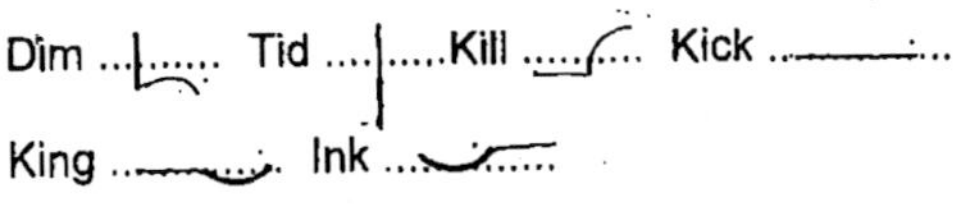

- Sound of long **"oo"** is represented by heavy dash (-)

Food ... Tool ... Pool ... Cool ...

Shoe ... Move ... Youth ... Tooth ...

Room ... Remove ... Route ...

- Sound of short **"oo"** is represented by light dash (-)

Book ... Took ... Look ... Hook ...

Hood ... Pull ... Cook ... Shook ...

For revision, please remember :-

<u>Note</u> The six long vowels are divided into dots and dashes vowels according to their pronounciation which are represented by the sentence **"PA MAY WE ALL GO TOO".** The six short vowels are represented by the sentence **"THAT PEN IS NOT MUCH GOOD".** We have already learnt that (i) In the beginning of the stroke - **<u>Ist Place</u>** (ii) In the middle of the stroke - **<u>IInd Place</u>** (iii) In the end of the stroke - **<u>IIIrd Place</u>**.

<u>Grammalogues/short forms</u>

A few very frequently used words are expressed in Shorthand by a single sign without giving vowel indication called grammalogues/short forms which promote speedy writing. All the learners may practise the same again and again and it should be thoroughly memorised -

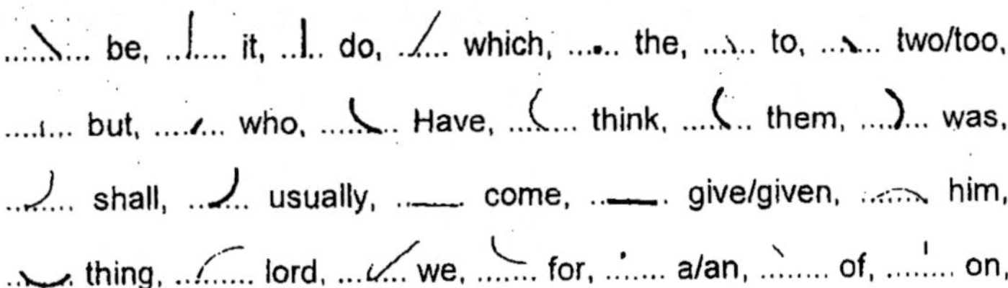

.... had, ... on the, ... but the, ...different/difference, ... wish, ... put, ... to be, ... owe, ... can, ... go, ... ought, ... in / any

****

PART - III DIPHTHONGS

The union of two vowels is called "Diphthongs" known as double vowels. There are four common diphthongs namely **i, oi, ow, u** as heard in the following sentence.

" I ENJOY GOW'S MUSIC "

It is also noted that **i, oi** and **ow** diphthongs are represented by angular mark .... and **'u'** diphthong is represented by semi-circle (.....). The sign of **'i'** (.......) and **'oi'** (........) are written at Ist Place of the consonant. The sign of **'ow'** (......) and **'u'** are written at IIIrd Place of the consonant.

Note: Learners may note that if the IIIrd Place diphthongs comes in between two strokes then the indication is placed before the IInd stroke as per the formula adopted earlier while placing the IIIrd place vowel **(See Part II).**

All the rules for diphthongs are the same as those of the vowels **(See Part II).** So they are to be treated / indicated just like first and third place vowels.

Type .... By .... Boy .... Toy .... Tie ....

My .... Shy .... Joy .... Enjoy .... Toil ....

Annoy .... Pie .... Admire .... Five .... Tire ....

Boiler .... Alloy .... Coy .... Dime .... Like ....

Out .... Loud .... Beauty .... Duty .... Outlook ....

Duke .... Cow .... Mouth .... Row .... Couch ....

Outlay .... Lounge .... County .... Cowed ....

Tube .... Bureau .... Cure ....

The difference for indication between vowel and diphthongs is that vowels are always indicated separately but, the diphthongs are sometimes joined in the beginning or at the end.

To obtain an easier outline, the diphthong signs are joined to the consonants, without lifting your pen/pencil, wherever convenient.

Idle .... Deny .... Few .... Value .... Oil ....

Due .... Jew .... Review .... Issue ....

Ice .... Eyes .... Renew .... Avenue ....

Grammalogues/Short Form

...... I /eye, ... how, ... why, ... beyond, ... you, ... with, ... when, ... what, ... would, ... me, ... owing

The following differences are there between Vowels and Diphthongs :

	Vowel	Diphthong
1.	Vowel is a single sound.	Diphthong is a union of two vowels means double vowels.
2.	Vowels are represented by dots & dash signs.	Diphthongs are represented by angular signs & semi-circles.
3.	Vowels are indicated separately.	Diphthongs are sometime joined in the beginning or at the end.
4.	Vowels are placed at Ist, IInd & IIIrd place.	Diphthongs are placed at Ist & IIIrd place.

****

PART - IV TRIPHONES

C

Triphone is a combination of **diphthong sound** and a **vowel sound** means combination of sounds of diphthong and vowel is called **Triphone.**

In other words, combination of three vowels sound together on one syllable is known as Triphones.

(Diphthong + One vowel = Triphone)

We have already learnt that the union of two vowels are called Diphthongs. If one of the **12** vowels immediately comes after a diphthong and the union becomes of three vowels, are called Triphones for which a small tick is added to the diphthong mark in the opposite direction.

- Buying .... Dying .... Loyal .... Fewer ....

  Tower .... Power .... Issuing .... Genuine ....

NOTE

(i) Triphones are slightly different from the Diphthong which generally create confusion in the minds of the learners that, whether the indication of Triphones is to be placed in some of the words or not. So, the learners may have to memorise the rules / procedures attentively to differentiate between the Diphthongs / Triphones.

(ii) We have seen that Diphthongs are represented by angular signs and the sign of semi circle whereas the vowels are represented by dots / dashes signs. Remember it carefully.

- **Phraseography**

The joining of two or more than two words written without lifting our pen/pencil is called **" Phrase "**. The outline, thus is called Phraseogram. The position of a phrase is determined from the position of the first word.

- In phraseography, **'I'** before **K, G, M, & L** is indicated by the initial tick e.g.

  I am .... I can .... I give .... I will ....

- Before all other strokes, it is indicated by the full sign of diphthongs e.g.

  I have .... I know .... I shall .... I think ....

- **L** stroke is represented for the word **"Will"** in phraseography e.g.

  It will .... Which will .... It will have ....

  It will be .... Which will be ....

- **P** stroke is represented for the word **"Hope"** in phraseography.

  I hope .... I hope you are .... I hope you will ....

****

PART - V CONSONANT (R)

The **R** consonant is written in two forms i.e. Upward form and Downward form in order to facilitate the joining with another stroke easily.

Upward R .... **Downward R** ....

- If a word is starts with **R** or it's sound, then **R** will be written upward and if the **R** is the first sounded stroke and preceded by vowel, then **R** will be written downward means; **a combination of "Vowel + R".**

  Rack .... Red .... Route .... Rug .... Ready ....

  Raw .... Retail .... Range .... Reach .... Road ....

  Air .... Arm .... Ear .... Oar ....

- If **R** is the last sounded stroke and ended with the sound of any vowels, then **R** will be written Upward otherwise Downward.

  Carry .... Memory .... Factory .... Dairy ....

Tomorrow .... Tarry .... Barry .... Injury ....

Bar .... Injure .... Car / Par .... Fair ....

- If the **R** comes in the middle, then **R** will be written Upward to give the better shape to the outline.

Park .... Party .... Mark .... Married .... Terrify ....

- But to attain the facile outline, **R** can be written downward also e.g.

Powerful .... Barely .... Clerk .... Tiresome ....

- If the **R** precedes **M** consonant, then **R** will be written downward

Arm .... Room .... Rome .... Remedy ....

- If **R** precedes **t, d, ch, j, th (ith), kl, gl** and **w,** it should be written Upward to secure facile outline e.g.

Artist .... Arch .... Urge .... Earth .... Ready ....

Regal .... Rewa .... Reach .... Writ ....

- Whenever there occurs three downward or three upward strokes in a word; **R** may be adjusted to attain two downward or two upward strokes.

It means after two upstrokes **R** will be written downward and after two downward **R** will be written upward e.g.

Prepare .... Posture .... Roarer ....

- If **R** follows ....(w), ...(y), ...**(h-upward)**, ...**(R-Upward)**, it should be written upward means if the **R** follows upward straight strokes then **R** is written upward e.g.

Rare .... Aware .... Yore .... Hurry ....

- **R** will be written upward if it follows **fs** or **ns** or straight horizontal or upstroke circled for (s) e.g.

Officer .... Answer .... Closer ....

Razor .... Wiser ....

- If **R** follows another stroke and is hooked finally, it is generally written Upward e.g.

Turn .... Burn .... Learn .... Return .... Portion ....

Grammalogues/Short Form

.... are (up), ... our or hour (up), ... and (up), ... should (up), ... your, ... year, ... whose, ... large, ... thank or thanked.

****

PART -VI CONSONANT - H

The **H** Consonant is also written in two forms :

.... **Downward form** .... **Upward form**

- If the **H** comes alone in a word or **H** comes with **K** (Kay) or **G** (Gay), it will be written downwards e.g.

He .... Hay .... Hoe .... Hake .... Haig ....

- Downward **H** is also written in the derivatives of words e.g.

Highly .... Higher .... Highway ....

(Derivatives = the word which is derived from another word)

- When **H** is joined to other consonants, **Upward H** is commonly used to obtain the better outline e.g.

Hood .... Heavy .... Hang .... Hitch ....
Huge .... Head .... Happy .... Hope .... Hotel ....

- When **H** follows Upward **L** or a horizontal stroke, it will be written downward e.g.

Lahore .... Cohesion .... Anyhow .... Unhook ....

- When **H** precedes **m, l, r** (downward) initially, **H** will be represented by a small tick instead of consonant e.g.

Home .... Hall .... Harm .... Healthy .... Hire ....

Whom .... Hello .... Help .... Hair ....

- When **H** comes in the middle and it is not convenient to write, then **H** will be represented by a light dot to follow the vowel e.g.

Apprehend .... Uphill .... Neighbourhood ....

Perhaps .... Likelihood .... Manhattan ....

- The word <u>**He**</u> in the middle or at the end of a phrase is represented by the short form .... e.g.

If he .... If he should .... If he can .... If he will be ....

Though he .... If he should be ....

- In other cases or in the beginning <u>**He**</u> is represented by full outline, e.g.

He will .... He will be .... He would be ....

He should be .... He may be ....

- The word hope is represented by stroke <u>P</u> to form the phrases; e.g.

I hope .... I hope you will .... I hope you are ....

We hope .... We hope you will .... We hope you are ....

****

PART - VII Small and Big Circle S / Z / SW

I SMALL CIRCLE

We have already learnt in the preceding lessons that the consonants **S / Z** are represented by .... but it is also represented by a small circle to make the speed in shorthand.

Therefore, in order to obtain easier and quicker outline, the sound of **S & Z** is represented by small circle. It is not called a consonant, so learners may note that the vowel indication is to be placed according to the initial consonant as per the rules & procedures adopted earlier.

- The **S** - circle is represented for the light sound of **S** in the beginning of a word.
- Initial sound of **Z** is represented by stroke **Z** instead of Circle - **S**.
- In the middle and at the end of a word, the **S** - circle is represented for light sound of **S** and heavy sound of **Z**.

The following are the examples.

Face .... Names .... Months .... Lose ....

Views .... Safe .... Slow .... Sales ....

Soon .... Salary .... Message .... Business ....

Reason .... Receive ....

Note: When joins to another stroke, the S-circle is written in two forms i.e. Left Motion means anti-clock wise motion and Right Motion means clock-wise motion. But mostly it is written with Left Motion.

- The **S** - circle should be written in the anti clock-wise motion when it is attached to any other straight stroke i.e.

i. It is written on the right side of straight down strokes means after the stroke

Copies .... Ladies .... Pages .... Spare ....

Speech .... Decide .... Sets .... Sit ....

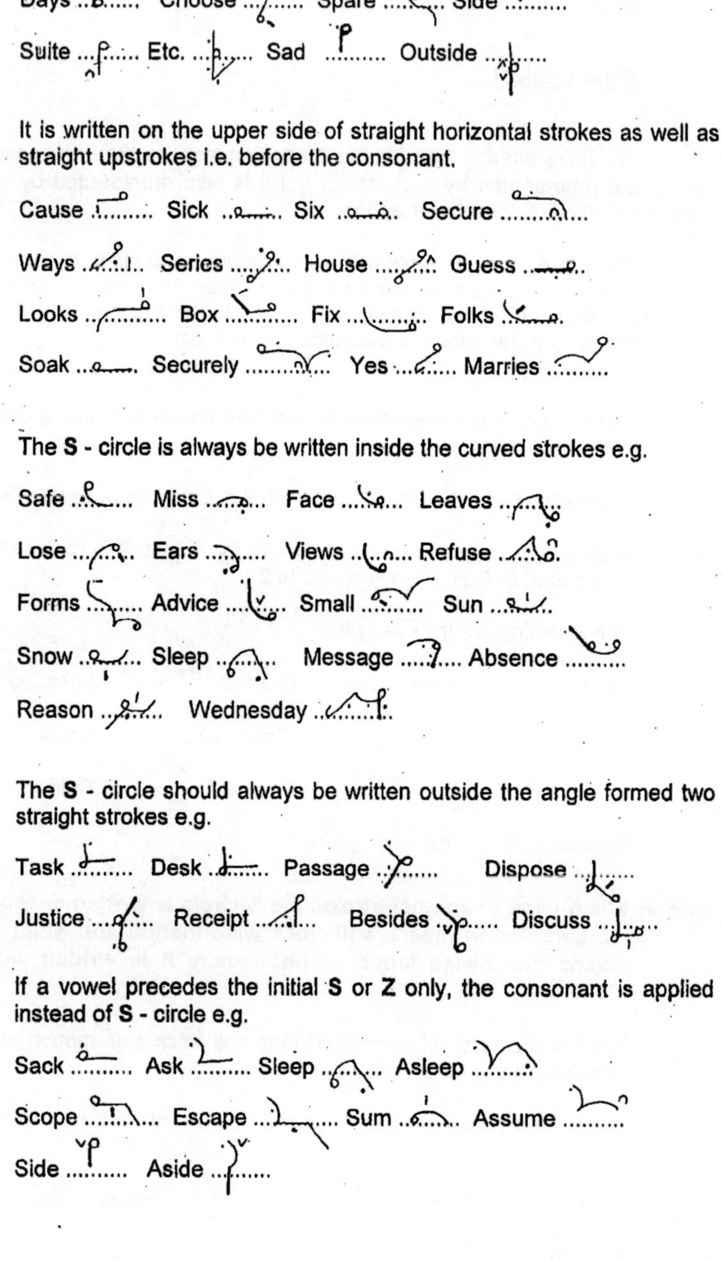

Days .... Choose .... Spare .... Side ....

Suite .... Etc. .... Sad .... Outside ....

ii. It is written on the upper side of straight horizontal strokes as well as straight upstrokes i.e. before the consonant.

Cause .... Sick .... Six .... Secure ....

Ways .... Series .... House .... Guess ....

Looks .... Box .... Fix .... Folks ....

Soak .... Securely .... Yes .... Marries ....

- The **S** - circle is always be written inside the curved strokes e.g.

Safe .... Miss .... Face .... Leaves ....

Lose .... Ears .... Views .... Refuse ....

Forms .... Advice .... Small .... Sun ....

Snow .... Sleep .... Message .... Absence ....

Reason .... Wednesday ....

- The **S** - circle should always be written outside the angle formed two straight strokes e.g.

Task .... Desk .... Passage .... Dispose ....

Justice .... Receipt .... Besides .... Discuss ....

- If a vowel precedes the initial **S** or **Z** only, the consonant is applied instead of **S** - circle e.g.

Sack .... Ask .... Sleep .... Asleep ....

Scope .... Escape .... Sum .... Assume ....

Side .... Aside ....

- If a vowel follows the final **S** or **Z** circle, the consonant is applied instead of **S** - circle e.g.

Busy .... Racy .... Rosy .... Policy .... Honesty ....

Lazy .... Modesty ....

- If a triphone precedes or follows only **S**, then consonant is applied e.g.

Science .... Sinuous .... Joyous .... Vacuous ....

- The circle also added to short form or grammalogues, e.g.

Haves .... Its .... Yours .... Speaks ....

Subjects .... Thanks .... Wishes .... Gives ....

Differences .... Puts .... Things .... Ours or Hours ....

- The small circle is represented for **'us'** in phraseography, e.g.

To us .... For us .... Of us .... Take us .... With us ....

Give us .... Show us .... Charge us ....

II Big Circle

In continuation of Small **S** - circle, a big Circle represents the **SW** (Sway) as well as **Ces, Ses, Sez** (CS, SS, SZ).

- Medially or finally, a small circle represents the sound of **S** or **Z** while a big circle represents the sound of **s's, c's, s'z** e.g.

Paces .... Cases .... Causes .... Boxes ....

Choses .... Necessary .... Successive ....

- Initially, a small circle represents the sound of **S** only while a big circle represents the sound of **SW** only.

Sweet .... Sweep .... Switch .... Swim ....

Swiftest .... Swayed .... Swear .... Swell ....

- If a vowel comes in between **s-s, c-s or s-z** the sign of vowels / diphthongs / triphones should be placed inside the big circle e.g.

Basis .... Census .... Resist .... Exhaust ....

Exist .... Exercise .... Insist ....

- In some of the cases, the initial bigger circle is represented for "as we" in the phraseography, e.g.

As we have .... As we shall .... As we think ....

As we know .... As we wish .... As we can ....

As we are ....

- When the word ends with a circle **(s)** and the next word starts with a circle **(s)** the bigger circle is used - it means that the large circle represents the two s's in phraseography, e.g.

This is .... This is the .... This city .... As soon as ....

As is .... As has ....

Note **The circle when standing alone should always be written in the anti-clock wise motion i.e. Left Motion.**

Grammalogues/Short forms

.... has/as, ... his/is, ... several, ... those, ... this, ... thus, ... because, ... special or specially, ... speak, ... subject or subjected, ... themselves, ... ourselves, ... as is, ... is as, ... myself, ... himself, ... itself, ... much, ... United States, ... New York, ... United States of America, ... especial-ly, ... language/owing, ... young, ... anything, ... nothing, ... something

****

PART VIII LOOP ST or STR

The sound of **ST** or **STR** is represented by small and big loops respectively written in the same direction as the **S** circle. The length of the small loop should be ½ of the stroke and that of big loop, should be 2/3 of the stroke. The initial loop is always read first and the final loop is always read at the last whereas the vowel signs are placed and read in relation to strokes.

Small loop .... for ST Big loop .... for STR

Like the **S - Circle**, the **ST** is written with the Left Motion (anti Clock-wise motion) to the straight strokes and inside the curve strokes, as shown below:

Seem .... Steam .... Sun .... Stone ....

Sake .... Stake .... Lace .... Laced ....

Base .... Based ....

The **STR** (Ster) loop is written with the left motion to straight strokes and inside curves as per the **S** - circle and the **ST** loop, as shown below:

Paster .... Faster .... Poster ....

Duster .... Chester .... Coaster ....

Roadster .... Investors ....

Note **STR loop is never written initially.**

Strong .... Strength ....

The **ST** loop represents either a light or heavy final sound i.e. zed / ced / sed when **ST** is written at the end but the word Caused .... is written full to distinguish from Cast ....

- If any vowel occurs in between **s-t** or **st-r**, then **ST/STR** loop is not applied in such words e.g.

Fast .... Facit .... Rest .... Receipt ....

Paster .... Pasture .... Best .... Beset ....

Opposed .... Opposite ....

- If the vowel comes after the final **ST** or **STR** loop, then **ST / STR** loop is not applied e.g.

Taste .... Tasty .... Honest .... Honesty ....

Paste .... Pasty .... Lace .... Lazy ....

Modest .... Modesty .... Police .... Policy ....

- The **S** - circle is always added on the opposite side of the loop means in continuation of **ST / STR** loop e.g.

Fasts .... Vasts .... Rests .... Tests ....

Posters .... Register .... Investors .... Masters..........

Note A small loop, half size of a stroke in length is used to represent the sound of st/sd. In case it is an initial sound or medial sound st loop is used for the sound of st only but in case of final sound it can be used for st/sd.

<u>Grammalogues/short forms</u>

.... largest, ... first, ... influence, ... influenced,

.... next, ... all,.......... though

****

<u>PART IX</u> <u>HALVING</u>

Whenever the length of any stroke is halved, there is an addition of **T** or **D** to that stroke means; halving a stroke in length indicates the addition of **T** or **D.**

In words of one syllable, a light stroke is generally halved for "**t**" and a heavy stroke for "**d**" only. But in words of more than one syllable, a stroke may be halved for either **t** or **d**.

Ply is called single syllable and **Apply** is called double syllable

Note .... Not .... Thought .... Wait ....

Yet .... Stopped .... Marked .... Checked ....

Reached ....

- To indicate a third position, a half length stroke is not written through the line, it should be written on the line by placing the IIIrd position vowel e.g.

East .... Feet .... Sheets .... Written ....

Invite .... Little .... Moved ....

- Where a final diphthong is joined, a stroke is generally halved to indicate a final **t** or **d**.

Doubt .... About .... Cute .... Issued ....

- Single syllable word having light or dark stroke with a final hook or a joined diphthong is halved for the addition of either **t** or **d**.

Meant or mend .... Tent or Tend ....

Proud .... Viewed ....

- **H** standing alone, if halved, should be written Upward only e.g.

High .... but Height .... He .... but Heat ....

<u>Note</u> **Learners may note that in the following cases, the halving principle is not employed.**

- To avoid any confusion with **should** (..........) & **and** (..........), the halving principle is not employed. So, we do not use **rt** .... and **rts** .... alone e.g.

Rate .... Rates .... Right .... Wrote .... Route ....

- Where the proper length of a halved stroke would not clearly show, the halving principle is not employed e.g.

Fact .... Effect .... Liked .... Select .... Territory ....

- Where a final vowel follows **t** or **d**, the halving principle is not employed e.g.

Pity .... Body .... Forty .... Window .... Into ....
Mighty .... Knotty .... Allottee ....

- **M, N, L** and **downward R** is halved only for **t**, not for **d**.

Met .... Neat .... Let .... Art ....

- The halving principle is not employed if by joining the two straight strokes and no angle is formed e.g.

Cooked .... Kicked .... Looked .... Judged ....

- If we want to add **"d"** to these strokes (**M, N, L and downward R**), then these strokes should be halved and thickened for **"d"** as shown as **md** .... **nd** .... **ld** .... **rd** .... (half length **ld** and **rd** must always be written downwards)

Made .... Need .... Old .... Aired ....

Moderate .... Middle .... Seemed .... Named ....

Ashamed .... Send .... Billed .... Mailed ....

World .... Filed .... Yield .... Installed ....

- When a vowel comes between **l - d** or **r - d**, the full stroke must be written instead of halving principle

Carried .... Delayed .... Followed .... Married ....

Valued .... Borrowed .... Worried ....

Means It is halved for **(d)** only when it is initially or finally hooked e.g.

Hampered .... Scampered .... Impugned ....

- To make the size accurately, half length **t** or **d** is always dis-joined when immediately following the strokes **t** or **d** thus;

Attitude .... Treated .... Credited .... Dictated ....

- In the past tenses - **ted** or **ded** is always indicated by half length **t** and **d** respectively thus;

Parted .... Braided .... Coated .... Graded ....

- Strokes **mp** .... **mb** .... **ng** .... should not be halved for the addition of either **t** and **d** unless they are initially or finally hooked thus;

Impute .... Imbued .... Belonged ....

but Hampered .... Rampant .... Lingered ....

Impugned ....

- Whenever the sign **rd** .... is not convenient to write then the sign **rt** may be used in place of **"rd"** and common sense be applied e.g.

Coloured .... Preferred .... Answered ....

- The signs for final **rt** and final **lt** are generally written Upward, but it is written downward after **N** and **NG** e.g.

Pilot .... Part .... Felt .... Start ....

Sort .... Skirt ....

but Inlet .... Ringlet .... Only ....

Unless .... Until ....

Grammalogues/Short Forms

.... quite, ... could, ... that, ... without, ... such,

.... wished

****

PART X - UPWARD AND DOWNWARD "L"

The **L** consonant is written in two forms i.e. Upward form and Downward form in order to facilitate the joining with another stroke easily.

Upward L .... **Downward L** ....

- **L** is generally written Upward as well as when it is standing alone e.g.

Load .... Delay .... Coal .... Fellow .... Sale ....

- When **L** follows **n** and **ng**, it should always be written downward e.g.

Only .... Kingly .... Mainly .... Wrongly ....

Recently .... Until .... Exceedingly .... Canal ....

Analysis .... Certainly .... Nelson ....

- **L** will be written in the same motion as that of the circle attached to a curve stroke to give the better shape means in continuation of the circle either Upward or Downward.

Pencil .... Lesson .... Vessel .... Losing ....

Nicely .... Council .... Noiseless .... Muscle ....

- If **L** comes initially, preceded by a vowel and followed by a horizontal stroke, it should be written downward and if a vowel does not precedes, **L** will be written upward i.e.

Alike .... Like .... Along .... Long ....

Elm .... Lime .... Allocate .... Locate ....

- After **f, v, sk** or a **straight upstroke (i.e. w, y, h, r)** and a vowel does not end the word, then **L** will be written downward. If a vowel follows **L**, then **L** should be written upward.

Fail .... Folly .... Fall .... Fellow .... Fool ....

Full .... Fully .... Successful .... Successfully ....

Rule .... Rely .... Avail .... Skill ....

- L is written downward initially when followed by **sv, sn, sng,** e.g.

Elusive .... Lesson .... Licence ....

Lessons .... Loosing ....

- L is written downward after **fs, vs, ns,** e.g.

Refusal .... Revisely .... Nicely .... Nestle ....

Pencil .... Council .... Cancel ....

- If **L** comes in the middle, it can be represented in both ways to attain the facile outline e.g.

Unload .... Unlock .... Facility .... Film ....

- A small initial hook, attached to stroke **L**, is represented for **W**. This hook is read first for **W** and then stroke e.g.

Wall .... Well .... Wealth .... Wealthy ....

Weld .... Will ....

- A large initial hook to **L** represents **Wh**. This hook is also read first before the stroke.

While .... Meanwhile .... Whale ....

Note There should not be any vowel before **Wh & W**. If vowel comes initially to **W & Wh** then stroke is to be written instead of **W & Wh** hook.

Grammalogues / Short Forms

.... inform-ed, ... never, November, ... satisfactory,

.... respect-ed, ... expect-ed, ... inspect-ed-ion,

.... January, ... February, ... together,

..........altogether, ... insurance

****

PART XI DOUBLE CONSONANT - STRAIGHT STROKES

(I) A small initial hook on the circle side means anti-clock wise motion of straight down strokes and straight horizontal strokes called double consonants. These double consonants are pronounced as **pel, bel, tel, del, chel, jel, kel and gel**. The vowels should be indicated as are placed to single consonant (**also see Part II**).

PL .... BL .... TL .... DL .... CHL .... JL ....

KL .... GL ....

Examples:

Placed .... Replace .... Blue .... Black ....

Total .... Entitled .... Enable .... Club ....

Replied .... Terrible .... Oblige .... Uncle ....

Duplicate .... Local .... Cloth ....

- If the **S** circle comes before the hook of **Pl** series, the **S** - circle is written inside the hook e.g.

Supply .... Split .... Settle .... Display ....

Physical ....

(ii) A small initial hook on the non-circle side means clock-wise motion of straight down strokes and straight horizontal strokes also called double consonants. These consonants are pronounced as **per, ber, ter, der, cher, jer, ker, ger.** The vowels should be indicated as are placed to single consonant.

PR .... BR .... TR .... DR ....

CHR .... JR .... KR .... GR ....

Examples:

Pray .... Presume .... Present .... Break ....

Trip .... Trust .... Drop .... Dry ....

Dress .... Grow .... Manager .... Increased ....

Note If an **initial circle (s / s's / sw)** or **loop - (st/str)** is written on the same side of the hook of **PR- series**, then it is pronounced with **initial circle** and **loop**. In the other words, if a circle on a loop is attached with a straight stroke with the right hand motion. It automatically covers **R**, e.g.

Suit .... Suitor .... Prey .... Spray ....

Stab .... Stabber .... Stitch .... Stitcher ....

Sweep .... Sweeper .... Switch .... Switcher ....

Seek .... Seeker .... Stick .... Sticker ....

Grammalogues/Short Forms

.... people, ... belief, believe, believed, ... tell, ... till, ... deliver-ed-y, ... call, ... called, ... equal or equally, ... equalled or cold, ... build/building (or able to), ... Doctor, ... dear, ... during, ... truth, ... principal, principally or principle, ... liberty, ... member, remember-ed, ... number or numbered, ... chair, ... cheer, ... care, ... description, ... surprise, ... surprised

****

PART XII DOUBLE CONSONANT - CURVE STROKES

A small initial hook on the inside of curve strokes are also forms a series of double consonants pronounced as **fr, vr, thr, nr** etc.

Friday .... Average .... Other .... Author ....

Shrink .... Leisure .... Favour .... Manner ....

Summer .... Farmers .... Efforts ....

- A large initial hook on the inside of curve strokes are called double consonants pronounced as **fl, vl, nl** etc.

Fly .... Flat .... Arrival .... Final ....

Original .... Personal .... Travel .... Privilege ....

(iii) The double consonants, as prescribed above, are also written in the reverse forms means opposite direction to the original form in the following cases :-

fr .... vr .... thr (ith) .... thr .... fl .... vl ....

a. When double consonants comes alone and the word does not begin with a vowel, then reverse form is to be used instead of original form e.g.

Free .... Fruit .... Three .... Through ....

Before **t, d, ch, j, n** and **ing**, original form is used as in

Friday .... Afraid .... Average.......... France.......... Frank ....

b. When double consonants are joined to another stroke, the forms are used either reverse or original which joins most conveniently. Mostly reverse forms are joined to the strokes written towards the right direction as it is easy to write the outlines in a proper way e.g.

Leather .... Brother .... Cover .... Forgot ....

Lever .... Discover .... Before ....

Means -- after **r (upward), w, y, h (upward), k, g, b & l (upward)** reverse form is used as in

River .... Weaver .... Clever .... Lover ....

Before .... Cover .... Leather .... Brother ....

Haver .... Heather .... Bother .... Gather ....

c. In continuation, **fl** and vl are also reversed after **k, g, n** and **straight upstrokes** e.g.

Rifle .... Naval .... Rival .... Reflect ....

Novel .... Cavalry ....

- The double consonant **Shl** is always written Upward and **Shr** consonant is always written downward.

Official .... Partial .... Speciality ....

Fisher .... Pressure ....

- The heavy sign .... is used to represent **ng-kr** or **ng-gr;**

Thinker .... Banker .... Stronger .... Finger ....

- **Grammalogues/Short Forms**

.... nor (or in our), ... near, ... own, ... owner, ... more, remark & remarked, ... remarkably, ...Mr. or mere, ... sure, ... pleasure, ... larger, ... largely, ... everything, ... over, ... however, ... respectfully, ... from, ... very, ... they are, ... their or there

****

PART XIII - SPECIAL USE OF DOUBLE CONSONANT

- The double consonant is used for the sake of attaining a facile outline, if the vowel occuring between the consonant and hook. A dot vowel may be indicated by writing a small circle instead of the dot either after or before the double consonant.

Parcel .... Darling .... Parlour .... Charm..........

- A dash vowel or a diphthong is shown by writing the vowel sign or diphthong sign through or at the beginning or end of the stroke.

Purchase .... Literature .... Attorney .... Tolerate..........

Nurse .... Moral .... Capture .... Lecture..........

Course .... Court .... Accordance ....

****

PART XIV - FINAL HOOK FOR - N and F/V

- A small final hook to all the straight strokes by the right motion means clock-wise motion represents the **N - hook.**

Pen .... Ten .... Chain .... Cane .... Gain ....

- A small final hook to all the straight strokes by the left motion means anti-clockwise motion represents the **F** or **V** e.g.

Puff .... Cave .... Tough .... Rough ....

- A small final hook written inside the curved strokes represents the sound of **N** e.g.

Fun .... Vain .... Line .... Nine .... Shine ....

Note There is no **F/V** hook to any curved strokes. Therefore in all such cases, **F/V** shall be represented by the consonants/strokes instead of hook.

Life .... Live .... Move .... Thief ....

- If a vowel follows final hook i.e. **F/V** or **N**, then the stroke is to be employed in order to indicate the following vowel.

Cough .... Coffee .... Pen .... Penny ....

Fun .... Funny .... Count .... County ....

- The **N** and **F/V** hook may be employed in between two strokes when they join easily and conveniently means medially **N** and **F/V** hook can be represented either by the hook form or by the stroke form as per convenience, e.g.

Agent .... Punish .... Defence .... Refer ....

Divide .... Attended .... Profit .... Prefer ....

Standing .... Agency .... Graphic .... Gravity ....

- In few cases, the strokes of **N** and **F/V** may also be employed instead of hook to secure a facile and easy outline e.g.

Wanted .... Printed .... Meantime .... Seconded ....

- If a sound of **S** or **Ses** or **St** or **Str** follows **N-hook** and attached to straight strokes then these attachments will be written on the same side of **N hook** viz. the right motion or clockwise motion and all the words will be pronounced with the sound of **N + circle/loop.**

Dan .... Dance .... Dances .... Dunster ....

Chance .... Bonds .... Accounts .... Returns ....

Once .... Against ....

- If a final small circle follows **F/V** hook attached to straight strokes, it will be written inside the **N-hook** e.g.

Proof .... Proofs .... Relative .... Relatives ....

Cave .... Caves .... Wave .... Waves ....

Advantage .... Advantages ....

- If a final sound of **NZ** follows a curve stroke, a small circle will be written inside the **N-hook** e.g.

Fines .... Lawns .... Mines .... Shines .... Earns ....

- But if the sound of **NS** follows curve strokes, it will be represented by **N-stroke + S circle** e.g.

Fence .... Essence .... Allowance ....

Romance .... Announces ....

Grammalogues/Short Forms

.... been, ... general-ly, ... within, ... southern, ... northern, ... opinion, ... represent-ed, ... representative, ... behalf, ... advantage, ... gentleman, ... gentlemen, ... can not, ... told, ... tried, ... trade - toward, ... third, ... difficult, ... difficulty, ... balance, ... balanced, ... responsible- ility, ... treat, ... guard, ... gold

****

PART XV SHAN HOOK - a large FINAL HOOK

- A large final hook written on the inside of all curve strokes is represented the syllable / sound of **"Shan"** and this hook is called Shan hook.

Fashion .... Motion .... Nation .... Attention ....

Admission .... Intention .... Supervision .... Session ....

- When attached to any straight stroke, **Shan** hook will be written on the opposite side to an initial circle or hook in order to preserve the balance of the outline e.g.

Station .... Section .... Expression ....

Hesitation .... Reception .... Discussion ....

Exception .... Anticipation ....

- **Shan** hook will be written with right motion if it is follows **fk** .... **fg** .... **vk** .... **vg** .... and it will be written with left motion if it is follows **lk** .... **lg** .... means the Shan hook is written far-away from the curve strokes to preserve the balance of the outlines e.g.

Fiction .... Vacation .... Affection ....

Vocation .... Location .... Selection ....

Legation ....

- **Shan** hook will be written on the right side when it is attached to straight strokes **t, d** and **j** e.g.

Notation .... Imitation .... Addition .... Magician ....

- When **Shan** is attached to simple straight strokes other than **t, d** and **j,** it will be written on the opposite side to the last vowel e.g.

Action .... Portion .... Operation .... Erection ....

Direction .... Obligation .... Deduction ....

Education ....

- When **Shan** follows the **S - circle** or **Ns** circle, it will be represented by a small hook or small curl on the opposite side of circle - means in continuation of the circle. If the third place vowel comes in between **S** and **Shan** it will be indicated outside the **curl / hook**.

Possession .... Taxation .... Opposition ....

Proposition .... Transition .... Position ....

- If a Triphone precedes a **Shan** sound, the stroke **Sh + N** Hook should be written. But to attain the shorter outline in some words, **Shan** hook may also be used e.g.

Extenuation .... Tuition .... Situation ....

Fluctuation .... Super-annuation .... Perpetuation ....

NOTE

(a) For the sake of plural - a small circle will be written inside the Shan hook e.g.

Occasions .... Nations .... Selections ....

(b) Shan hook is also written in between two strokes e.g.

Additional .... National .... Intentional ....

Transitional ....

Grammalogues/Short Forms

.... information, ... public/publish/published, ... publication, ... object or objected, ... objection, ... organise or organised. .... organisation, ... satisfaction, ... investigation, ... yesterday.

****

PART XVI ABBREVIATED & MEDIAL (W)

- The stroke of W is not convenient in joining with some of the strokes. So, at the beginning of **k, g, m & R** (downward & upward), a small initial **semi - circle** is used as an abbreviation for w, as shown :

Weak .... Wig .... Worry .... Womanly .... Walk ....

Were .... Wear .... Worked .... Worst .... Worm ....

- The small **semi - circle** is always read first. When a vowel begins a word, the stroke w.......... Is to be written instead of **semi - circle**.

Wake .... Awake .... Ware .... Aware ....

We have already seen that a right **semi - circle** is used initially for **(w) before k, g, m & R**(up & down), when it is not preceded by a vowel. But when the stroke **(w)** cannot easily be joined with the preceding stroke in the middle, it is represented by writing a disjoined **semi - circle** with the left or right motion.

Left Motion : A left semi - circle represents **(w)** followed by a dot vowel, e.g.

Farewell .... Twenty .... Twelve ....

Herewith .... Overwhelming ....

Right Motion : A right semi - circle represents **(w)** followed by a dash vowel, e.g.

Misquote .... Guesswork .... Woodwork ....

Sea-wood ....

****

PART XVII - COMPOUND CONSONANT

The consonants, which give two sounds at a time, are called compound consonants means whenever two consonants immediately follow each other (without a vowel in between) they are called compound consonants.

- A large initial hook attached to **K** or **G**, the consonants **K** and **G** are called **Kwa** and **Gwa**.

Linguist .... Quoted .... Sanguine ....

Quarter .... Quantity .... Requested .... Require ....

Quick .... Requisite .... Quest ....

Whenever **M** is thickened, the new consonant called **mp & mb**.

Jump .... Camp .... Thumb .... Tomb ....

Dump .... Lump .... Campaign .... Embody ....

Note Initial or final hook can be attached to **mp / mb** e.g.

Lumber .... Dampen ....

Whenever downward **L** is thickened, the consonant represented for **Ler**. Thickened form of **Ler** is written in the derived words and written downward only e.g.

Full .... Fuller .... Feel .... Feeler ....

Dwell .... Dweller .... Rule .... Ruler ....

Scale .... Scholars .... Counsel .... Counsellor ....

Whenever downward **R** is thickened, the consonant represented for **Rer**. Thickened form of **Rer** is also written in the derived words and written downward only e.g.

Bear .... Bearer .... Fair .... Fairer ....

Admire .... Admirer .... Share .... Sharer ....

Hire .... Hirer .... Wear .... Wearer ....

Poor .... Poorer .... Clear .... Clearer ....

Note If the vowel comes after **Ler** and **Rer**, full outline is to be written.

When **M** is immediately followed by **pr, br, pl** or **bl**, the double consonants .... are to be used instead of thickened **M**.

Impress .... Embrace .... Imply .... Emblem ....

If the hook of **W** is enlarged, the new consonant represents the sound of **Wh**.

Whistle .... Where .... Everywhere .... Whisper ....

Grammalogues/Short Forms

.... whether, ... important/ce, ... improve, improved-ment, ... impossible, ... child, ... chaired, ... cheered, ...accord-ing (or according to), ...cared, ... particular, ... opportunity, ... short, ... hand, ... under, ... yard, ... word, ...immediate, ... school, ... schooled, ... spirit, ... certificate, ... knowledge, ... acknowledge

****

PART XVIII - DOUBLING PRINCIPLE

Curved strokes are doubled in length to indicate the sound of **tr, dr, ther** and **ture** e.g.

After .... Father .... Centre .... Sister ....
Future .... Natural .... Entertain .... Interview ....
Elevator .... Orders .... Folder .... Another ....

Straight strokes are also doubled in length to indicate the sound of **tr, dr, ther** and **ture** when it follows (i) another stroke, (ii) circle s, (iii) finally joined diphthong or (iv) a final hook e.g.

Chapter .... Director .... Operator .... Scatter ....
Powder .... Painter .... Renders .... Typewriters ....
Educator .... Refrigerator .... Picture ....

Note Straight stroke standing alone is never doubled for **ter, der** and **ther.** Only the sound of **ter** will be added when the stroke **L** is doubled. **Final circle - s** is added for plural only. Full outline is to be adopted for **der, ther** etc.

Letter .... Letters ....

but Leader .... Older .... Better .... Gather ....

Weather .... Readers ....

- There will be an addition of **-er** when stroke **mp / mb** is doubled. The doubled form will be pronounced as **mpr / mbr.**

Bumper .... Timber .... Jumper ....

Note Learners may note that in the following cases, the doubling principle is not employed.

- Doubling principle is not employed for making the past tenses of any word. At this stage, halving principle should be adopted

Wonder .... Wondered .... Enter .... Entered ....

Order .... Ordered .... Centre .... Centred ....

- When a vowel follows final **tr, dr, thr** etc., doubling principle is not employed.

Anger .... Angry .... Inventor .... Inventory ....

- For the addition of light sound of **ther**

Panther .... Arthor ....

Grammalogues/Short Forms

.... character, ... wonderful or wonderfully, ... rather or writer, ... therefore, ... interest

****

PART XIX - PREFIXES

A prefix is a common syllable occuring at the beginning of words.

- Initial **con-com** is expressed by a light dot written first at the beginning of the following stroke. The outline is to be written according to the 1st sounded vowel after the prefix **con-com.**

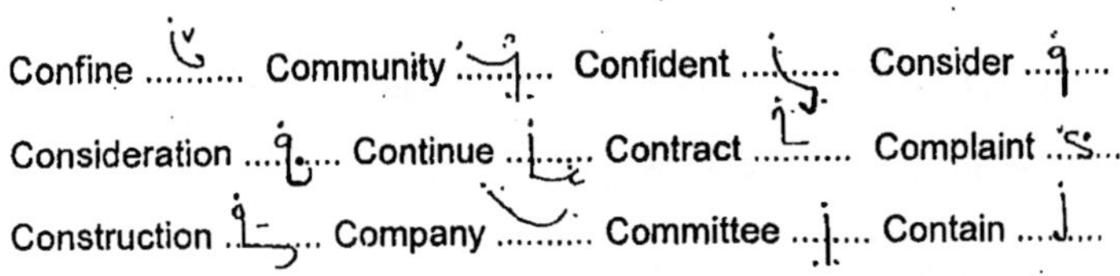

Confine .... Community .... Confident .... Consider ....

Consideration .... Continue .... Contract .... Complaint ....

Construction .... Company .... Committee .... Contain ....

- But in certain words, it is convenient to write the prefix full e.g.

Commission .... Commerce ....

- In the middle of a word or phrase, **con-com** or **cog** is expressed by writing the two strokes close to each other e.g.

Recommend .... Mis-conduct .... Dis-connect ....

Reconsider .... Circumscribe .... Dis-continued ....

Welcoming .... Incomplete .... Recognition ....

Recognise .... In this connection .... I am compelled ....

You will be compelled .... I am confident ....

Note : Cum and **Cun** in the beginning is never represented by dot, e.g.

Cumbersome .... Cunning ....

- Initial **Accom-accommo** is expressed by joined or disjoined **K** and the outline is always to be written at the 1st place as the 1st sounded vowel in **Accom-accommo** is **"Short a"** (**1st Place Vowel**)

Accomplish .... Accommodate ....

Accommodation .... Accompany ....

- Initial **Intro** is expressed by disjoined double length **ntr** .... The outline is always to be written in the third position because the 1st sounded vowel in **Intro** is **"Short - i"** (**IIIrd Place Vowel**) .

Introduce .... Introducing .... Introspect ....

- Initial **Magna-Magne-Magni** is expressed by disjoined **M**. The outline is always to be written in the 1st position because the first sounded vowel in **Magne-Magne-Magni** is **"Short a"** (**1st Place vowel**)

Magnetise .... Magnify .... Magnifier ....

Magnitude .... Magnificent ....

- Prefix **Self** is represented by a disjoined **S-circle** close to the following stroke in the second place vowel. The outline will always be written in the 2nd place because the 1st sounded vowel in **Self** is of **2nd place.**

Self defence ...... Self satisfied .... Self made ......

Self feeder .... Self reliance ....

Self + Con / Com is expressed by a disjoined **S-circle** written at the place of **con / com** dot. There is no need to place the dot of **con-com.** The outline will always be written in the **2nd position.**

Self contained ....Self control .... Self confident ....

Self complacent ....

In- before **str, skr, Upward H** is represented by a small hook written in the clockwise direction. As the 1st sounded vowel in "IN" is of 3rd place, the outline is to be written in the 3rd position.

Instrument .... Inscriber .... Inhabit .... Instruct ....

Inherent ....

- The small hook for **"IN"** should not be used in the case of negative words, it is always expressed by the stroke **"N"**.

Inhospitable .... Inhumanity.......... Inhuman...........

- **Trans-** In the beginning it is generally represented by contracting the outline by omitting n, e.g.

Transfer .... Transport .... Translate .... Transmit ....

Transplant .... Transcribe ....

But if there is a vowel between **trans** - and the follow - **consonant**, the n is not omitted, e.g.

Transit .... Transact .... Transaction ....

****

PART XX - SUFFIXES

A suffix is a common syllable occuring at the end of a words.

- Where it would be awkward to write **ing** .... at the end of a word, the suffix **ing** is represented by a light dot.

Requesting .... Ordering .... Meeting .... Serving ....

Assisting .... Morning .... Wanting ....

- Light dot for **NG** will be written in the following cases :-

After Downward **R,** light straight downstroke and short form e.g.

Teaching .... Assuring .... Getting .... Paying ....

Interesting .... Securing .... Replying .... Trying ....

Coming .... Thinking ....

- **Ing** is represented by a final dot for singular and **ings** for plural is represented by a final light dash e.g.

Meetings .... Settings .... Switchings ....

Mornings .... Learnings ....

Note In the middle of a word, **NG** stroke for **"ing"** is to be used instead of light dot.

- Where the sign of **mnt** .... can not be easily joined, the suffix **ment** is represented by half **nt** ....

Achievement .... Consignment .... Commencement ....

- The suffix **mental-mentally** and **mentality** are represented by disjoined **ment** e.g.

Experimental .... Departmental ....

Sentimental .... Fundamental ....

- The endings **fulness** and **lessness** are indicated by disjoined **Fs**....... and **Ls** .... respectively.

Thoughtfulness .... Carefulness .... Hopefulness ....

Thoughtlessness .... Carelessness .... Hopelessness ....

- The suffix **ship** is expressed by a joined or disjoined **Sh** .... which joins conveniently.

Friendship .... Leadership .... Scholarship ....

Hardship .... Citizenship .... Membership ....

- The suffix **Logical-ly** are expressed by disjoined **J** ....

Psychological .... Physiological .... Biological ....

- The word **-ward** and **-yard** are expressed by half length **W** and **Y** respectively.

Forward .... Backward .... Backyard ....

Forwarding ....

- **Lity - rity - arity - ality** and other similar terminations are expressed by disjoining the preceding stroke means disjoining the stroke coming before the termination to the other remained stroke.

Formality .... Possibility .... Inability ....

Liability .... Majority .... Minority ....

Similarity .... Regularity ....

Grammalogues/Short Forms

.... commercial-ly, ... inscribe-d, ... inscription, ... instructive, ... instruction, ... circumstance, ... signify-ied or significant, ... significance, ... govern-ed, ... government, ... advertise-d-ment, ... regular, ... probable-ly-ility, ... individual-ly, ... prospect, ... whatever, ... whenever, ... sufficient-ly-cy

****

PART XXI - DIPHONES

When the two consecutive vowels pronounced in two separate syllables are represented by the angular signs .... These signs are called **Diphones.**

The first sign .... represents a **dot vowel** followed by any other vowel and the second sign .... represents a **dash vowel** followed by any other vowel. The signs are written in the place of the first vowel of the combination.

Examples for first sign ....

Payable .... Saying .... Material ....

Obvious .... Medium .... Real ....

Convenient .... Agreeable .... Glorious ....

Courteous .... Seeing ....

Examples for second sign ....

Co-operate .... Co-operation .... Following ....

Drawing .... Growing .... Knowing .... Lower ....

Showing ....

The following are the differences between Diphthongs & Diphones :

	Diphthongs	**Diphones**
1.	Diphthong is a combination of two vowels in one syllable.	Diphone is a combination of two vowels in different syllables.
2.	In diphthong, there are four Signs.	In diphones, there are two signs.
3.	Diphthongs are marked in the first & third places only.	Diphones are marked in all the three places.
4.	Diphthongs are joined to the strokes.	Diphones are not joined to the strokes.

Grammalogues/Short Forms

.... danger, ...financial-ly, ... mortgage-ed, ...

neglect-ed, ... practice/practise-d, ... university, ...

English, ... exchange-d, ... familiar-ity, ... telegram

****

PART XXII - INTERSECTIONS

When we write one stroke through another stroke is called intersection which is used for the brief in a short way as well as an indication of official titles etc.

Note **Where intersection is impracticable, the method of writing one stroke in close proximity to another stroke is to be adopted as mentioned in the following list.**

- **P consonant** is represented for **Party.**

Conservative Party	....	Janta Party	....
Political Party	....	Parliamentary Party	....
Party Bill	....	Labour Party	....

- **B consonant** is represented for **Bank** or **Bill.**

City Bank	....	Bank Rate	....
Finance Bill	....	Education Bill	....

- **T consonant** is represented for **Attention.**

Early Attention	....	Necessary Attention	....
Finance Attention	....	Education Attention	....
Careful Attention	....	Special Attention	....

- **D consonant** is represented for **Department.**

Government Department	....	Foreign Department	....
Municipal Department	....	Shipping Department	....
Electrical Department	....	Engineering Deptt.	....

- **CH consonant** is represented for **Charge.**

This Charge .... Free of Charge ....

- **J consonant** is represented for **Journal.**

Banker's Journal .... Journal of Commerce ....

Journal of Education .... School Journal ....

- **K consonant** is represented for **Company, Capital, Council** and **Captain.**

Delivery Company .... This Company ....

Authorised Capital .... Capital Charge ....

Captain of the Ship .... Ship's Captain ....

Cabinet Council .... Privy Council ....

<u>Note</u> We also used the consonant **K** with **N hook** for the word **Council** instead of **K** stroke to avoid any confusion.

- **G consonant** is represented for **Government.**

British Government .... Government Official ....

Of the Government .... Janta Government ....

<u>Note</u> **G** with **N hook represents Beginning e.g.**

At the beginning ....

- **F consonant** is represented for **Form.**

Necessary form .... Medical form ....

- **TH (ith) consonant** is represented for **Authority & Month.**

Legal Authority .... Local Authority ....

Well known authority .... Government Authorities ....

For a month .... In a month's time ....

How many months .... Next Months ....

- **S consonant** is represented for **Society.**

Agricultural Society .... Medical Society ....

- **M consonant** is represented for **Manager, Morning, Mark and Major.**

General Manager .... Sunday Morning ....

Auditor's Mark .... Major General ....

Note To avoid confusion in the words **Manager** and **Major, we may use M** with **N hook** for **Manager.**

- **N consonant** is represented for **National.**

National Affair .... National Bank ....

National divided .... National Society ....

- **L consonant** is represented for **Liberal and Limited.**

Liberal Party .... Liberal View ....

Jackson Limited .... Pear's Limited ....

- **R (Downward) consonant** is represented for **Arrange-d-ment.**

I shall arrange .... Please make arrangements ....

We have arranged ....

- **R (Upward) consonant** is represented for **Require-d-ment, Railways.**

Do you require .... You may require ....

You will be required .... Your requirements ....

To meet the requirements .... Railway Ticket ....

Railway Official .... Railway facilities ....

- **PR double consonant** is represented for **Professor.**

Professor Jackson .... Professor of Politics ....

Grammalogues/Short Forms

.... inconvenience-t-ly, ... distinguish-ed, ... income, ... become, ... becoming, ... welcome, ... nevertheless

****

PART XXIII - FIGURES

In dealing with round figures the following method is adopted, otherwise, the figures are represented by shorthand outlines.

- Stroke .... (n) for hundred.

500 .... 700 .... 900 ....

- Stroke .... (ith) for thousand.

5,000 .... 9,500 ....

- Stroke .... (m) for million.

5 million .... 10 million ....

- Stroke .... (b) for billion.

5 billion .... 15 billion ....

****

Short Forms

List-I & II containing all short forms/grammalogues with indication or distinctive outlines for similar words.

SHORT FORM

The following short forms, as given in **List - I & II**, are for the words that are very frequently used and promote speedy writing and it should thoroughly be practised and memorised by the learners / high speed aspirants.

- All the learners / high speed aspirants may select the forms which are distinctive and legible at sight.

- If one short form consisting of two words or more and the outlines are the same, the learners may mark their own indication to differentiate the outlines to avoid any awkward position during transcribe the passage.

LIST - I

A or an	....	
Accord-ing	....	.... or
Acknowledge	....	
Advantage	....	
Advertise-d-ment	....	....
All	....	
Altogether	....	
Aught	....	
Awe	....	
And (up)	....	
Any	....	
Anything	....	
Are	....	
As	....	
As is	....	

Balance ....

Balanced ....

Be ....

Because ....

Become ....

Becoming ....

Been ....

Behalf ....

Belief-ve-d .... or ....

Beyond ....

Build-ing ....

But ....

Call ....

Called ....

Can ....

Can not ....

Care ....

Cared ....

Certificate ....

Chair ....

Chaired ....

Character ....

Cheer ....

Cheered ....

Child
Circumstance
Cold
Come
Commercial-ly ... or
Could
Danger
Dear
Deliver-y-ed ... or
Description
Different-ce ... or
Difficult
Difficulty
Distinguish-ed ... or
Do
Doctor, Dr.
During
English
Equal-ly ... or
Equalled
Especial-ly ... or
Everything
Exchange-d ... or ... or
Expect-ed ... or
Eye

Familiar-ity

February

Financial-ly

First

For

From

General-ly

Gentleman

Gentlemen

Give-n

Go

Gold

Govern-ed

Government

Great

Guard

Had

Hand

Has

Have

He

Him

Himself

His

Hour

How

However

Immediate

Important-ce

Impossible

Improve-d-ment

In

Income

Inconvenience-t-ly

Individual-ly

Influence

Influenced

Inform-ed

Information

Inscribe-d

Inscription

Inspect-ed-ion

Instruction

Instructive

Insurance

Interest

Investigation

Is

Is as ....

It ....

Itself ....

January ....

Knowlege ....

Language ....

Large ....

Largely ....

Larger ....

Largest ....

Liberty ....

Lord ....

Me ....

Member ....

Mere ....

More ....

Mortagage-d .... or ....

Most ....

Mr. ....

Much ....

Myself ....

Near ....

Neglect-ed .... or ....

Never ....

Nevertheless ....

New York ....

Next ....

Nor ....

Northern ....

Nothing ....

November ....

Number-ed .... or ....

Object-ed .... or ....

Objection ....

Of ....

On ....

Opinion ....

Opportunity ....

Organization ....

Organize-d .... or ....

Ought (down) ....

Our ....

Ourselves ....

Over ....

Owe ....

Owing ....

Own ....

Owner ....

Particular ....

People ....

Pleasure ....

Practic(s)e-d ....

Principal-ly .... or

Principle ....

Probable-ly-jility- .... or or

Prospect ....

Public ....

Publication ....

Publish-ed .... or or

Put ....

Quite ....

Rather ....

Regular ....

Remarkable ....

Remark-ed .... or ....

Remember-ed .... or ....

Represent-ed .... or ....

Representative ....

Respect-ed .... or ....

Respectful-ly ....

Satisfaction ....

Satisfactory ....

School ....

Schooled ....

Sent ....

Several ....

Shall ....

Short ....

Should (up) ....

Significance ....

Significant ....

Signify-ied ....

Something ....

Southern ....

Speak ....

Special-ly ....

Spirit ....

Subject-ed ....

Sufficient-ly-cy ....

Sure ....

Surprise ....

Surprised ....

Telegram ....

Tell ....

Thank-ed ....

That ....

The ....

Their ....

Them ....

Themselves ....

There ....

Therefore ....

Thing ....

Think ....

Third ....

This ....

Those, Thyself ....

Though ....

Thus ....

Till ....

To ....

To be ....

Together ....

Told ....

Too ....

Toward ....

Trade ....

Tried ....

Truth ....

Two ....

Under

United States

University

Usual-ly

Very

Was

We

Welcome

What

Whatever

When

Whenever

Whether

Which

Who (Down)

Whose

Why

Wish

Wished

With

Within

Without

Wonderful-ly .... or

Word

Would

Writer

Yard

Year

You

Young

Your

Yesterday

LIST II

Administrator

Administratrix

Amalgamate

Amalgamation

Arbitrary

Arbitrate

Arbitration

Arbitrator

Appointment

Architect-ure-al ... or ... or

Assignment

Abandonment

Attainment

Bankruptcy

Capable

Certificate

Character

Characteristic

Circumstantial

Cross-examination

Cross-examined

Contentment

Contingency

Commercial-ly

Defective

Deficient-ly-cy

Denomination-al

Description

Discharge-d

Dangerous

Deliverance

Demonstrate

Demonstration

Destruction

Destructive

Destructively

Efficient-ly-cy

Electric
Electrical
Electricity
Emergency
England
English
Englishman
Enlarge
Enlargement
Enlarger
Entertainment
Enlightenment
Enthusiastic-iasm
Especial-ly
Esquire
Establish-ed-ment
Executive
Executor
Executrix
Expediency
Expenditure
Expensive
Extinguish-ed
Exigency
Falsification
Familiar-ity

Familiarization

Familiarize

February

Financial-ly

Govern-ed

Government

Generalisation

Henceforward

Howsoever

Identical

Identification

Immediate

Imperfect-ion-ly

Imperturbable

Incandescence

Incandescent

Inconsiderate

Inconvenience-t-ly

Incorporated

Independent-ly-ce

Indispensable-ly

Individual-ly

Influential-ly

Inform-ed

Informer

Inspect-ed-ion

Insurance

Intelligence

Intelligent-ly

Intelligible-ly

Interest

Introduction

Investigation

Investment

Irrecoverable-ly

Irregular

Irremovable-ly

Irresponsible-ility

Irrespective

Irrespectively

January

Jurisdiction

Justification

Knowledge

Legislative

Legislature

Magnetic-ism

Manufacture-d

Manufacturer

Manuscript

Mathematical-ly ... or

Mathematician

Mathematics

Maximum

Mechanical-ly ... or

Messenger

Metropolitan

Minimum

Ministry

Misfortune

Monstrous

Mortgage-d ... or

Neglect-ed ... or

Negligence

Never

Nevertheless

Nothing

Notwithstanding

November

Objectionable

Objective

Obstruction

Obstructive

Oneself

Organisation

Organize-d

Organizer

Parliamentary

Passenger

Peculiar-ity

Perform-ed

Performance

Performer

Perpendicular

Perspective

Practicable

Practice

Practise-d

Prejudice-d-ial-ly

Preliminary

Probable-ly-ility

Productive

Production

Proficient-ly-cy

Project-ed

Proportion-ed

Proportionate-ly

Prospectus

Prospective

Public

Publication

Publish-ed

Publisher

Questionable-ly

Ratepayers

Recoverable

Reform-ed

Reformer

Regular

Relinquish-ed

Remarkable-ly

Remonstrance

Remonstrate

Removable

Represent-ed

Representation

Representative

Reproduction

Republic

Republican

Respective

Respectively

Responsible-ility

Retrospect

Retrospection

Retrospective

Satisfactory

Selfishness

Sensible-ly-ility

Signification

Something

Stranger

Stringency

Subjective

Subjection

Subscribe-d

Subscription

Substantial-ly

Sufficient-ly-cy

Suspect-ed

Sympathetic

Telegram

Telegraphic

Thenceforward

Thankful-ly

Together

Unanimity

Unanimous-ly ....

Uniform-ity-ly ....

Universal-ly .... or ....

Universality ....

Universe ....

University ....

Unprincipled ....

Valuation ....

Whatever ....

Whenever ....

Whensoever ....

Whereinsoever ....

Wheresoever ....

Whithersoever ....

Yesterday ....

****

Brief, Tips and Procedure

Brief & some important tips on "How to achieve your target in Stenography.

BRIEF AND SOME TIPS FOR SHORTHAND LEARNERS/HIGH SPEED ASPIRANTS

Stenography is, perhaps, the only course of study where high percentage or higher qualification is not essential or necessary. Instead of acquiring higher qualification, good knowledge of stenography is enough to acquire a job in the field. The results of competitive examinations conducted for recruitment in Government, Public or Private Sectors as also the results of ITIs, YWCA, Employment Exchanges and other Government Organisations suggest that the candidates with even secondary level qualification have managed to secure very good marks compared to those with higher qualifications. However, for learning stenography and to become a perfect stenographer, the essential ingredients are command over the language, regular practice, zest for learning, punctuality, good general knowledge and sharp memory.

It has been widely observed that the learners get dis-heartened either in the initial or in the middle stage of learning stenography. I realised that the largest number of drop outs in stenography learning was due to many factors related to teaching and understanding of the subject as other language. Many regret it as a boring subject compared to other subjects. This happens owing to the lack of adequate guidance, concentration, dedication, interest in the subject and above all zeal to achieve their goal. Remember that sincerity and keenness helps for achieving the goals and, therefore, shorthand learning is no exception. Only, the sincere and enthusiastic aspirants pursue the complete training and achieve their desired goal.

The author of this book has experience of over a decade of lecturing on various facets of the subject and confident that if the following guidelines/principles are followed by the learners, the process of learning would become much easier:

- Acquire full knowledge of rules and established principles of stenography. Mere theoretical knowledge or low speed in shorthand does not help in achieving the desired results. Therefore, in the first instance, the essential requirement is to master the textbook which will help in laying good and strong foundation. If a stenographer is not master of theory or the fundamentals, he/she can not formulate the easy and convenient outlines.

- The meaning, importance, objectives, proof history of shorthand, its scope, employment opportunities and future prospects should also be explained to all the learners/high speed aspirants to motivate them for the target alongwith the benefits from its proper learning.

- High speed can be achieved only and only through regular practice. Some of the students gets tired in the mid of the course with the result their efforts just go in vain. Therefore, the learners are well advised that practice should not be suspended at any cost and they can retain that speed only with regular practice. Learners / high speed aspirants should remember that regular practice makes a man perfect as their success lies in honest, planned and systematic practice.

- The role of Stenography Instructor is of very high significance in the field. The Learner/high speed aspirants should rely on Instructors who possess good command over the language having a clear, distinct and metallic voice with correct pronunciation.

- Voice and pronunciation familiarization are important factors. To acquire these, the learners/high speed aspirants may take dictation from fellow students, friends or anybody who is capable of dictating any passage as this procedure of rotational practice helps in familiarizing with different type of voices and pronunciation. To familiarize yourself with correct pronunciation, consult a standard language dictionary as the words are pronounced differently by different people hailing from different States.

- In normal work situations, a stenographer confronts fluctuations in dictation. To cope with such a situation, during practice, the passage should fluctuate at different levels in the following manner: first minute at 80 words per minute, next two minutes at 100 words per minute, next four minutes at 120 words per minute, next two minutes at 100 words per minute and the last minute at 80 words. This method of practice helps them to avoid any problem while taking down the dictations having fluctuations at different levels.

- The dictation passages should be wide and varied in order that the students get acquainted with difficult words, terminologies and phrases used in different fields i.e. Parliamentary debates, newspaper editorials, commerial and financial reviews, AGM reports of business houses and reports of various Committees and Commissions. So this form of ideal passages must be used for dictation passages to cover all the difficult words and terminologies.

- The outlines should neither too small nor too big but of medium size. Medium size of outlines helps to make single/halving/double length strokes clearly distinguishable. Difficult/awkward outlines should be checked attentively and noted in a separate note-book for convenience.

- A good stenographer should be able to transcribe the dictated passage @ speed of 40-50 words per minute. This is possible only if the Learners have normal typing speed of 60 words per minute. Errors in transcription should be checked by comparing it with the original dictated passage and also ensure that the errors are less than one per cent as a good transcription required command over the language and proficiency in typing. A regular practice of transcription makes one more confident to face the examinations.

- While transcribing the shorthand passage, punctuations to the extent possible, should not be avoided. So, since beginning, marks of punctuation are always be used to be a perfect stenographer.

- While taking down the dictation passage, do not think of other things. Think only of what you are writing having concentration as also the **"sense"** of the matter/dictation material.

- Repeated practice of a single passage helps in recognizing and memorizing the difficult words/awkward outlines to which one often stumbles while taking dictation. It also helps in enhancing the speed with accurate outlines. This method of practice helps in developing manual dexterity of a high order.

- Another way of familiarizing with typical outlines is by reading the dictated shorthand passages preferably loudly by all the Learners/high speed aspirants. It has been noticed that a large number of students shies away from shorthand reading. Reading the shorthand passage play a pivotal role in stenographic art. So, I would suggest that every learner/high speed aspirants should read the printed shorthand passage(s) regularly to familiarize with the difficult/awkward outlines and its meaning. It also helps in enhancing the speed with accurate outlines.

- Phraseogram/Grammalogues should be clear, distinct, legible and should not clash with any other words. It should not include any difficult or unfamiliar words. The learners/high speed aspirants should first master all the phrases/grammalogues, otherwise, they will not be able to write them at the speed stage. So, my advice to all the Learners/high speed aspirants that they must have to keep at first to the principles of phrasing/grammalogues to acquire the shorthand speed perfectly in a short time.

- The students should have the knowledge of all significant consonants, characters of shorthand, one word/two word, hyphenated words, pair of words, foreign words, legal words, phrases, contractions, grammalogues etc. To achieve highest speed with accuracey - eagerness, devotion, sincerity and intelligence is desirable.

- It is only an accomplishment and reward of long arduous industry to become a perfect stenographer having years of consistent and persistent practice and sometimes in the face of repeated failures. So, Learners/high speed aspirants have to be very patient as they are well known that practice has become second nature and the collection, analysis and assimilation of fresh contractions, phraseograms and joinings are the preliminary factors having sincerity of interest in the course if they want to achieve their target/goal.

After taking into consideration of all the above guidelines/procedures by the learners/high speed aspirants, the standard of efficiency may put them in the following categories:

Percentage of Errors	Category
Without mistake	Outstanding
Less than 1%	Excellent
Between 1% to 2%	Very Good
Between 2% to 3%	Good
Between 3% to 4%	Satisfactory
Between 4% to 5%	Average
More than 5%	Failed

****

Pair of words

Meaning with sentence and its distinctive outlines for similar words.

PAIR OF WORDS

The following words are likely to be confused because they are quiet similar in sound or meaning and some of these words have the same form or origin. It is, therefore, necessary that learners/high speed aspirants should try to understand their precise meaning so as to avoid any confusion during transcribe the dictated shorthand passage. In addition, self-made indication as well as prescribed vowels are also to be used to dinguish its outline and meaning for convenience.

Words	Outline	Meaning
Accept	....	Agree to - I accept the terms of your offer.
Except	....	To exclude - I wish to except the clause calling for repayment of the deposit.
Access	....	Way of approach or entry.
Excess	....	Over & Above the limits.
Alter	....	To change.
Altar	....	Worship Place - Table used in a Christian Service
Allowed	....	Permitted.
Aloud	....	Loudly, not silently.
Angle	....	Space between two meetings, corner lines.
Angel	....	Attendant or Messenger of God.
Adopt	....	To take an idea or method, legally take another child's as one's own.
Adapt	....	Become adjusted to new conditions.
Advice (n)	....	Recommendation about future action or behaviour.
Advise (v)	....	Give advice to, inform.

--	**Adverse**	....	Opposite, unfavourable - The dry weather has had an adverse effect on the Garden.
	Averse	....	Disliking - is related in origin and also has the sense of opposed but is usually employed to describe a person's attitude e.g. I would not be averse to making the repairs myself.
--	**Affect**	....	To cause a change, good or bad.
	Effect	....	Result produced, consequence.

Both **affect and effect** are verbs and nouns, but only effect is common as a noun usually meaning **"as a result, consequence, impression"** etc., e.g. - **My father's warnings had no effect on my adventurousness**. As verbs they are used differently. Affect means **"to produce an effect upon"**, e.g. - **Smoking during pregnancy can affect the baby's development**. Effect means, **"to bring about"** e.g. - The negotiators effected an agreement despite many difficulties.

--	**Amicable**	....	Showing or done in a friendly way.
	Amiable	....	Agreeable, Lovable, Likable, Sweat
--	**Apposite**	....	Suitable, well expressed, well chosen.
	Opposite	....	Contrary, Different having a position on the other side.
--	**Assent**	....	Express, Agreement, Consent or sanction especially for officials (usually followed by - to)
	Ascent	....	Act of going up, upward slope, progressing.
--	**Avenge**	....	To give just punishment.
	Revenge	....	To give punishment in return for an injury, win after earlier defeat, inflict retaliation for an offence or injury.

--	**Accede**	....	Absent or agree
	Exceed	....	Be more or greater than, surpass.
--	**Assay**	....	Difficult attempt, testing of a metal or ore to determine its ingredients and quality.
	Essay	....	A piece of written composition.
--	**Avocation**	....	Hobby or casual occupation.
	Vocation	....	One's regular employment or occupation, strong feeling of fitness for a particular, career in religious contexts.
--	**Abject**	....	Degraded, miserable, wretched, abasing.
	Object	....	Express or feel opposition, dis-approval or reluctance, protest.
--	**Abatement**	....	Make or become less, strong, severe.
	Abetment	....	To help in an evil deed, encourage or assist.
--	**Altogether**	....	Totally.
	Alltogether	....	In one group.

Altogether - totally, completely, on the whole in total.

Altogether and **All together** are used in different contexts - **Altogether** means in total e.g., - The Hotel has twenty rooms altogether. **Altogether**, I have five years on the island. **All together** means **"all at once"** or **"all in one place or in one group"**, e.g. - The packages arrived all together. We managed to get three bedrooms all together

--	**Allusion**	....	Indirect reference.
	Illusion	....	A deceptive appearance, misapprehension of the true state of affairs.

--	**Apprehend**	....	Seize, arrest / understand - perceive.
	Comprehend	....	Include, grasp mentally, understand/ including all or nearby all.
--	**Bail**	....	Money as security for the temporary release of a person in custody.
	Bale	....	Bundle, make-up trial into bales.
--	**Bad**	....	Mohan is a bad boy.
	Bed	....	She is lying in bed.
--	**Born**	....	I was born in Delhi.
	Borne	....	He has borne many difficulties in his life.
--	**By**	....	She goes to School by bus.
	Buy	....	I want to buy this Book.
--	**Birth**	....	Give birth to, to come into existence, origin.
	Berth	....	Sleeping place for.
--	**Bare**	....	Unclothed, naked, uncovered, leafless.
	Bear	....	Carry, bring.
--	**Bridal**	....	Relating to wedding.
	Bridle	....	Headgear, to control a horse / an animal.
--	**Beside**	....	At the side of, near, compared with.
	Besides	....	In addition to, apart from.
--	**Break**	....	Make or become in-operative, to destroy, separate into pieces.
	Brake	....	Device for stopping or slowing a vehicle.
--	**Bore**	....	Make a hole especially with a revolving tool, tiresome or dull person.
	Boar	....	A wild pig.

--	**Blew**	To make sound by playing an instrument, past of blow.
	Blue	Colour.
--	**Cattle**	The cattle are grazing in the field.
	Kettle	The kettle on the stove.
--	**Card**	He writes a post card to his father.
	Cord	Tie this bundle with a cord.
--	**Canvass**	Canvassing especially of electors, trying to secure votes.
	Canvas	Strong coarse, rough cloth, kind of cloth used for sails and tents etc. as a surface for oil painting.
--	**Caste**	An exclusive class, Hindu hereditary class.
	Cast	Throw especially deliberately or forcefully, make a product in this way.
--	**Confidant (n)**	One to whom secrets are confided, Person trusted with knowledge of one's private affairs.
	Confident (adj.)	Feeling or showing confidence, certain.
--	**Cannon**	A big heavy gun installed on a carriage.
	Canon	General Law, rule or principle.
--	**Council**	Assembly, Advisory, Deliberative or Administrative Body.
	Counsel	Give advice on personal problems especially - professionally.
--	**Coarse**	Rough or loose in texture or grain, made of large particles.
	Course	Path, ground on which a racket etc. takes place, series of lessons in a particular subject.

--	**Choir**	....	A Group of Singers esp. taking part in Church services.
	Quire	....	Twenty four sheets of paper.
--	**Complements**	....	Thing that completes.
	Compliments	....	Regard, polite expressing of praise, congratulates, formal greetings.

Complementary means - forming a complement or addition, completing - I purchased a suit with a complementary tie & handkerchief. It can be confused with complimentary for which one sense is **'given freely, as a courtesy'** - You must pay for the suit, but the tie and handkerchief are complimentary.

--	**Cite**	....	Quote a passage in support, mention in an official dispatch.
	Sight	....	The power of seeing, range of vision.
	Site	....	This is the new site of our office.
--	**Corpse**	....	Dead body
	Corps	....	A division of Army, Body of people engaged in a special activity.
--	**Calender**	....	A roller machine in which cloth, paper etc. is rolled to glaze or smooth it.
	Calendar	....	A table showing months/dates, time table of appointments, special events.
--	**Censor**	....	An official who examines, written matters, motion pictures, news to suppress any parts on the grounds of obscenity security etc.
	Censure	....	Condemnation or strong disapproval, harsh criticism.
--	**Career**	....	One's advancement through life esp. in course of life.
	Carrier	....	One that carries like truck etc.

--	**Concert**	....	Musical performance, combination of voices or sounds.
	Consort	....	A husband or wife, spouse esp. of Royalty, Group of Players.
--	**Ceiling**	....	Inner roof, upper limit.
	Sealing	....	Decorative adhesive stamp, fastening with seals, attached to a document as a guarantee of authenticity or security.
--	**Cemetery**	....	A burial place/ground.
	Symmetry	....	Harmony, correct or beautiful, proportion of parts facing each other.
--	**Session**	....	Assembly of a deliberative or judicial body to conduct its business, academic year.
	Cession	....	Act of ending (or rights, property and esp. of territory by a nation.
--	**Check**	....	To control & verify, examine the accuracy, quality or conditions of.
	Cheque	....	Written Order for money in a Bank.
--	**Collision**	....	Violent impact of a moving body with another or with a fixed object or clushing of opposed interests or considerations, dashing together.
	Collusion	....	Secret, fraudulent agreement, conspire together, secret plan to commit a crime.
--	**Complacent**	....	Self satisfied.
	Complaisant	....	Agreeable, willing to please, acquiscent.

Complacent means - Smugly, self satisfied - After four consecutive championship the team became complacent. **Complaisant** a much rarer word means **'deferential, will to please'** - Once released from the pen, the barking dogs became peaceful and complaisant.

--	**Conscience**	....	Moral sense of right or wrong.
	Conscious	....	Awake & aware of one's surroundings and identity, the conscious mind.
--	**Dairy**	....	Store where milk & milk products are sold.
	Diary	....	Daily record of events & thoughts.
--	**Drought**	....	The crops failed owing to drought, Prolonged absence of rain.
	Draught	....	I drank the medicine at one draught, Quantity drunk at a time.
	Draft	....	It is a draft on the State Bank.
--	**Decent**	....	Avoiding obscenity, respectable, acceptable, good enough.
	Descent	....	Act or way of discending, downward slope, decline, fall.
	Dissent	....	Disagreement, differ esp. from established or official opinion, difference of opinion, non-conformity.
--	**Defer**	....	Postpone.
	Differ	....	Disagree, be unlike or distinguishable.
--	**Deference**	....	Courteous regard, respect, compliance, sent - in deference to out of respect for.
	Difference	....	Quantity by which amounts differ, disagreement, not the same.
--	**Defy**	....	Challenge a person to do or prove something, resist openly, refuse to obey.
	Deify	....	Regard or worship, as a God.

--	**Dependent**	Person who depends on another for financial support.
	Dependant	Relying on, reliable.
--	**Desert**	Uncultivated, barren sandy region.
	Dessert	Sweet course at the end of dinner.
--	**Device**	Thing mad or adapted for a particular purpose, Plan, Scheme or Trick (s) leave a person to his/her own devices.
	Devise	To make a Plan or invent carefully.
--	**Dual**	Dual ownership, double, two-fold.
	Duel	Armed contest between two persons, any contest between two.
--	**Dose**	Single portion of medicine, quantity of something experienced e.g. Work, Praise, Punishment etc.
	Doze	Light Sleep, behalf asleep.
--	**Dear**	Beloved or esteemed - Baby is dear to me.
	Deer	An animal - I saw many deer in the Zoo.
--	**Due**	Owing or payable.
	Dew	Moisture from air in small drops between night & morning.

Due process - Legal procedures to ensure individual rights. **Due to** - **'Because of'** as in - We were late due to circumstances beyond our control. **In due course** - at about the appropriate time in the natural order.

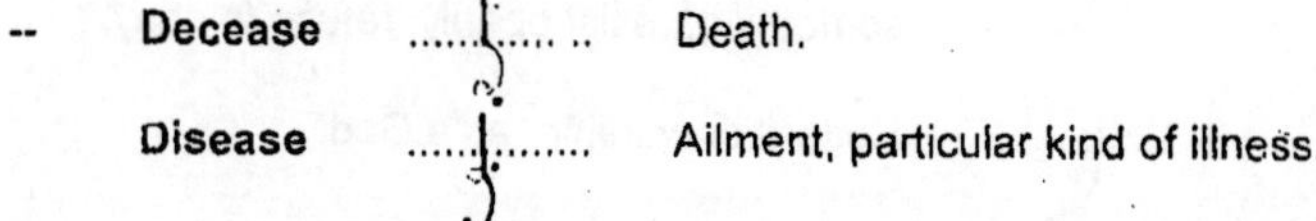

--	**Decease**	Death.
	Disease	Ailment, particular kind of illness.

--	**Dying**	....	To die / death.
	Dyeing	....	To colour.
--	**Eligible**	....	He is eligible for this Post, Fit or entitled to be chosen, desirable esp. for marriage.
	Illegible	....	Your handwriting is illegible, can not be read, not legible.
--	**Envelop**	....	To wrap up or cover completely.
	Envelope	....	Folded paper container usually with a sealable flap, for a better.
--	**Emerge**	....	To come up or out into view, become recognised or prominent
	Immerse	....	To plunge into, sub-merge a person, absorb or involve deeply.
--	**Extent**	....	Scope, size, degree, space over which a thing extends.
	Extant	....	Still existing.
--	**Elusive**	....	Evasive, difficult to remember, difficult to find or catch.
	Illusive	....	Unreal deceptive, misapprehension of the true state of affairs.
--	**Equable**	....	Uniform, even, tranquil
	Equitable	....	Just, fair.
--	**Eminent**	....	Notable, High in rank, distinguished.
	Imminent	....	Impending, about to happen, threatening to occur immediately.
	Immanent	....	Inherent, indwelling.

Eminent means **"Outstanding famous"** - The book was written by an eminent authority on folk art. Imminent means **"about to happen"** - People brushed aside the possibility that was imminent. Immanant often used in religious or philosophical contexts, means inherent - He believed in the immanent unity of nature taught by the Hindus.

--	**Elicit**	....	To draw out, evoke (a response etc.)
	Illicit	....	Unlawful, forbidden, secret.
--	**Emigrate**	....	To leave one's own country to settle in another.
	Immigrate	....	Come as a permanent resident into a country, person who immigrates.
--	**Envy**	....	To be unhappy on the achievement on the others.
	Envious	....	Full of envy.
	Envoy	....	Messenger or representative, diplomat ranking below Ambassador.
--	**Exalt**	....	Praise highly, raise in rank or power, make rapturously excited.
	Exult	....	Be joyful, to rejoice.
--	**Exhausting**	....	Tiring, consume or use up the whole of, tire-out.
	Exhaustive (Adj.)	....	Comprehensive, thorough.
--	**Errand (N)**	....	Short outing for a specific purpose, task, message, some light duty.
	Errant (Adj.)	....	Mistaken, wandering, deviating from an accepted standard.

	Word	Outline	Meaning
--	**Fair**	....	Beautiful, Just, Festival, in accordance with the rules.
	Fare	....	Passenger paying charges to travel in a public vehicles.
--	**Facility**	....	Ease conform equipment or resources for doing something.
	Felicity	....	Intense happiness.
--	**Fain**	....	Willing under the circumstances to, gladly.
	Feign	....	Pretend, stimulate.
--	**Factitious**	....	Contrived, artificial, not natural.
	Fictitious	....	Unreal, Imaginary, Not genuine.
--	**Farther**	....	At a greater distance (Nothing was farther from his thoughts. - The falls were still two or three miles farther up the path.
	Further	....	Greater in degree or quality, in addition (We decided to consider the matter further.)
--	**Feet**	....	I have two feet, plural of foot.
	Feat	....	The juggler showed many feats, A deed of skill, noteworthy act or achievement.
--	**Funeral**	....	Burial or cremation of a dead person with its ceremonies.
	Funereal	....	Sad, Gloomy dismal.
--	**Formerly**	....	Previously, in former times.
	Formally	....	Ceremoniously, Convention, explicit or official (formal agreement)
--	**Flower**	....	Part of a plant from which the fruit or seed is developed, blossom.
	Flour	....	Meal or powder obtained by grinding grain esp. Wheat, any fine powder.
	Floor	....	Any ground surface.

--	**Foul**	....	Dirty, offensive, against the rules.
	Fowl	....	Domestic birds esp. chickens kept for eggs.
--	**Farmer**	....	Peasant.
	Former	....	Of the past, earlier, previous.
--	**Gate**	....	Shut the gate, An entrance or exit, door, barrier.
	Gait	....	She has a charming gait, Manner or walking or running.
--	**Gaol**	....	Jail, Prison.
	Goal	....	Aim, Object of a person's ambition or effort.
--	**Gentle**	....	Mild Polite. not rough.
	Genteel	....	Fashionable, graceful in form, upper-class.
--	**Gamble**	....	Play games or chance for money, bet.
	Gambol	....	Skip/frolic - Playfully, cheerful play.
--	**Here**	....	Sit here.
	Hear	....	I can not hear your voice.
--	**Herd**	....	I saw a herd of cattle in the field.
	Heard	....	I have heard your story.
--	**Heart**	....	Do not lost heart, Organ which makes blood circulate.
	Hart	....	A kind of Deer.
	Hurt	....	He was hurt in the accident.

--	**Hare**		A timid animal, mammal like a large rabbit.
	Hair		As covering of man's head, fine threadlike strands growing from the skin of mammals esp. from the human head.
--	**Honorary**		Holding an office without receiving salary.
	Honourable		Worthy of honour.
--	**Hew**		To cut or chop with an ax, sword cut into shape (A block or wood)
	Hue		Colour, A shade of colour.
--	**Human**		Pertaining to man, human being
	Humane		Kind, Benevolent, Compassionate.
--	**Heel**		Hinder part of show, back part of the foot below the ankle person regarded with contempt and disapproval, lean over at one side.
	Heal		Cure, make well, become sound & healthy again.
--	**Ideal**		Answering to one's highest conception, perfect or supreme excellent, moral principle or standard of behaviour.
	Idle		Without work, lazy, indolent, unemployment.
	Idol		Image of a deity etc. as an object of worship.
--	**Inconstant**		changeable, irregular
	Inconsistent		Having self contradictory parts.
--	**Ingenious**		Skilful, cleverly contrived.
	Ingenuous		Simple, innocent, frank

--	**Impassable**	....	Those which can not be crossed.
	Impossible	....	That which can not be accomplished, not easy, not possible.
	Impassible	....	Incapable of feeling or emotion, incapable of suffering injury.
--	**Insight**	....	Capacity of understanding.
	Incite	....	In instigate, urge.
--	**Impudent**	....	Disrespectful, impertinent.
	Inprudent	....	Unwise, rash, indiscreet.
--	**Lose**	....	Become unable to follow, be deprived of, fail to gain.
	Loose	....	No tight, free from bonds or restraint.
--	**Lesson**	....	Part of course of teaching, systematic instruction.
	Lessen	....	Make or become less, diminish, abate, reduce.
--	**Lightening**	....	Make or become lighter in weight, making less, reduce the weight or load.
	Lightning	....	Flash or bright light produced by an electric discharge between clouds or' between clouds and the ground.
--	**Later**	....	Comparative degree of 'late', after the due, usual proper time.
	Latter	....	Coming after, refers to position second mentioned of two.
	Letter	....	Post this letter.
--	**Loan**	....	Anything lent esp. money, person who lends money at exorbitant rates of interest.
	Lone	....	Solitary, without a companion.

	Word	Outline	Meaning
--	**Loathe**	....	Hate, detest.
	Loath	....	Unwilling, dis-inclined, reluctant.
--	**Lead**	....	Direct the actions or opinions of, go through, to guide.
	Lead	....	A metal.
--	**Liar**	....	Person who tells a lie esp. habitually.
	Lawyer	....	Professional expert in law.
--	**License (v)**	....	To permit, grant licence to.
	Licence (n)	....	Permission
--	**Mail**	....	It is a mail train.
	Male	....	She has no male issue.
--	**Modal**	....	A piece of metal with inscription used as a reward.
	Meddle	....	Interfere in or busy oneself unduly with other's concerns.
--	**Moral**	....	Principle of right and wrong conduct.
	Morale	....	Spirit of fortitude or endurance, mental attitude or bearing of a person or group esp. as regards, confidence, discipline.
--	**Marshal**	....	Officer of a judicial district, high ranking officer in armed forces.
	Martial	....	Brave in fighting, Warlike, brave.
--	**Mantel**	....	The ornamental shelf, above and around fire place.
	Mantle	....	A kind of cloak, loose sleevless cloak.
--	**Marry**	....	To wed, unite intimately.
	Merry	....	Full of joy, be festive, enjoy oneself.

	Word	Outline	Meaning
--	**Metal**	....	Any of a class of chemical elements such as gold, silver, iron and tin.
	Mettle	....	Strength of character, spirit, courage.
--	**Meet**	....	To come face to face with, fit, suitable (of two or more people come together or into contact with)
	Meat	....	Animal flesh as a food.
--	**Minor**	....	Lesser, under-age or comparatively small in size or importance.
	Miner	....	One who works in a mine.
--	**Main**	....	Chief in size, importance.
	Mane	....	Long hair on the neck of horse and lion etc.
--	**Naughty**	....	Badly behaved disobedient.
	Knotty	....	Difficult, puzzling (knotty problem)
--	**None**	....	Nobody
	Nun	....	Woman living in convent under religious vows.
--	**Ordnance**	....	Branch of the armed forces dealing esp. with military stores & materials, military weapons.
	Ordinance	....	A rule or order, authoritative order, decree.
--	**Oar**	....	Pole with a blade used for rowing or steering a boat by leverage against the water, of a boat.
	Ore	....	Mineral
--	**Pray**	....	To ask
	Prey	....	Victim, hunted by another animal that is hunted or killed by another for food.

--	**Prosecute**	....	Institute legal proceedings against (a person)
	Persecute	....	Subject to hostility or ill treatment esp. on the grounds of political or religious belief.
--	**Physic**	....	Medicine
	Physics	....	Science dealing with the properties, one of the branches of science.
	Physique	....	Bodily structure, build.
--	**Proscribe**	....	Prohibit, ban.
	Prescribe	....	Advise the use of (a medicine etc.) recommend of impose authoritatively, lay down.

Prescribe and **Proscribe** are sometimes confused but they are nearly opposite in meaning - **Prescribe** means **"to advise the use of"** or impose authoritatively whereas **Proscribe** means **"to denounce or ban"** e.g. (i) Our teacher prescribed topics to be covered. (ii) The doctor prescribed a painkiller. (iii) The Principal proscribed tabloid newspapers from the School Library. (iv) A totalitarian regime may prescribe some books and proscribe others.

--	**Proceed**	....	Continue, go on with an activity, so farward.
	Precede	....	Come or go before in time, order, importance
--	**Pain**	....	Trouble, range of unpleasant bodily sensations produced by illness, accident etc.
	Pane	....	A sheet of glass in a door or window.
--	**Petrol**	....	Refined mineral oil used in motor car.
	Patrol	....	Act of walking of travelling around an area in order to protect or supervise it.

-- **Pair** — A set of two persons or things used together.

Pare — Trim by cutting away the surface or edge, to cut, diminish little by little.

-- **Piece** — A small portion, each of the parts of something, collapse emotionally.

Peace — A state of calm, quiet, freedom from or cessation of war.

-- **Pail** — Bucket, amount contained in this.

Pale — Whitish appearance, become feeble in comparison (with).

-- **Personal** — Private, one's own, individual.

Personnel — Body of persons - employees involved in a public, undertaking or armed forces.

-- **Plain** — Clear, evident, simple, not attractive, uncomplicated, unembellished.

Plan — Scheme or procedure by which a thing is to be done, diagram.

-- **Pour** — Flow or cause to flow esp. downward, dispense (a drink) by pouring.

Pore — Small hole, be absorbed in studying.

-- **Practice (n)** — Doing a thing repeatedly, habitual action or performance, professional work or business of a doctor or lawyer.

Practise (v) — To do a thing again and again.

-- **Precedent** — Previous case or legal decision etc. taken as a guide for subsequent cases or as a justification, an example which may be following afterwards.

President — Chairman, Presiding Officer, Elected Head of a Republican Government.

	Word	Outline	Meaning
--	**Profit**	....	Advantage or benefit, financial gain.
	Prophet	....	Religious seer or interpreter, one who can see into the future, Spokesman, Advocate.
--	**Prophecy (n)**	....	Prediction of future events.
	Prophesy (v)	....	To foretell future events, speak as a prophet.
--	**Propose**	....	To make a suggestion, put forward for consideration or as a Plan.
	Purpose	....	Object to be attained, thing intended, resolution, determination.
--	**Quiet**	....	Keet quiet
	Quite	....	I am quite well.
--	**Root**	....	Basic cause, source, origin.
	Route	....	The course followed in a journey, way or course taken (esp. regularly)
--	**Ring**	....	I have lost my ring.
	Wring	....	Wring out the towel.
--	**Respectful**	....	Full of respect, showing deference (Stood at a respectful distance)
	Respectable	....	Decent and proper in appearance and behaviour, fairly competent, worthy of respect.
	Respective	....	Particular person or thing.
--	**Rain**	....	Moisture falling in drops from clouds.
	Reign	....	Period of rule, sovereignty period during which a sovereign rules.
	Rein	....	A long narrow strap attached to the bit of a bridle, means of control, to restrain.

--	**Roll**	....	Move or go in some direction by turning as an axis, to take attendance, call one by one.
	Role	....	Part, function, actor's part in a play. (She played a role of heroine)
--	**Right**	....	Morally or socially correct, not mistaken.
	Rite	....	Religious or solemn observance, act or procedure.
	Write	....	Write in ink.
--	**Rays**	....	Narrow beam of light from a small or distant source, straight line in which rediation travels to a given point.
	Raze	....	Destroy completely, tear down.
--	**Rows**	....	Lines.
	Rose	....	A beautiful flowers, light pinkwine.
--	**Redress**	....	Set right, redressing (a grievance etc.)
	Re-dress	....	Put on cloth again, rectify.
--	**Remark**	....	Said again, say by way of comment, written or spoken comment.
	Re-mark	....	Mark again.
--	**Residents**	....	Those who live.
	Residence	....	Dwelling
--	**Read**	....	To study something.
	Reed	....	Various marsh or water plans (The vibrating sound producing part of the mouthpiece of some wind instruments.)
--	**Recover**	....	Regain, get back.
	Re-cover	....	Cover again.

--	**Sensual**	....	Appealing to the based senses, sensual feelings, pleasing to the senses.
	Sensuous	....	Easily affected by the medium of the senses, derived from the senses.
--	**Soar**	....	To fly high without using power.
	Sore	....	Of a part of the body painful, sore place on a body, distressing.
	Sour	....	The grapes are sour.
--	**Sail**	....	Piece of material extended on rigging to catch the wind and proper a vessel of a ship, travel on water by the use of sails and engine power.
	Sale	....	To sell.
--	**Soul**	....	Spiritual entity, Spiritual or immaterial part of a human being.
	Sole	....	Under-surface of the foot (The sole of my shoe is worn-out), single, exclusive.
--	**Spacious**	....	Having a lot of space.
	Specious	....	False, though seemingly true.
--	**Soot**	....	Black powdery deposit from smoke. The chimney is full of soot.
	Suite	....	Set of rooms in a hotel, set of things belonging together.
	Suit	....	Set of clothes for a special occasion, lawsuit. The climate of this place does not suit me.
--	**Steal**	....	To take without permission, illegally in secret.
	Steel	....	Metal

	Word	Outline	Meaning
--	**Stair**	....	Indoor steps, the set of fixed steps for ascending.
	Stare	....	Looking fixedly with eyes open esp. as a result of curiousity, surprise etc. to gaze intently.
--	**Stationary**	....	Motionless, not meant to be moved.
	Stationery	....	Writing material such as Pens, Paper etc.

> Be careful to distinguish **Stationary** - **"not moving, fixed"** **Stationery** - **"Writing paper and other supplies".**

	Word	Outline	Meaning
--	**Statue**	....	Case image of a person or animal.
	Statute	....	Written law of the legislature.
--	**Story**	....	Account of imaginary or past events, tale, narrative.
	Storey	....	Horizontal division of a house.
--	**Straight**	....	Direct without curve or bend.
	Strait	....	A narrow passage of water between two seas / oceans / large bodies of water.
--	**Tamper**	....	To meddle with, to make unauthorised changes in a document.
	Temper	....	Disposition of mind, irritation, anger.
--	**Tail**	....	Of an animal, a rear extension.
	Tale	....	Story or narrative esp. fictitious, gossip.
--	**Temporal**	....	Worldly as opposed to spiritual, secular, pertaining to the time in this life or this world.
	Temporary	....	Short lived, person employed, temporarily.

--	**Team**	....	A group of players.
	Teem	....	Be full of (teeming with ideas), be abundant
--	**Urban**	....	Situated in a city or town (opp. rural)
	Urbane	....	Smooth, polite, courteous, elegant and refined in manner.
--	**Vain**	....	Ostentatious, Idle, Fruitless, Conceited.
	Vein	....	Any blood vessel, anyof the tubes by which blood is conveyed to the heart.
	Vane	....	Weather cock, an appliance for showing the direction in which the wind blows.
	Wane	....	To decrease, diminish, become weaker.
--	**Veil**	....	A covering, a thin cover used - The bride raised her veil.
	Vale	....	Valley, a low ground between hills. - The vale of Kashmir is very beautiful.
--	**Vacation**	....	Holidays, away from home for pleasure and recreation.
	Vocation	....	Profession, person's employment.
--	**Veracious**	....	True, speaking the truth.
	Voracious	....	Greedy in eating, ravenous, very eager.
--	**Venal**	....	Able to be bribed or corrupted, mercenary.
	Venial	....	Pardonable, capable of being forgiven or excusable.
--	**Very**	....	Same, true, actual.
	Vary	....	Make different, modify, diversify

--	**Waste**	....	Make or become weak, which is of no use. - Do not waste your money.
	Waist	....	Part of the body between hips and ribs. - She was wearing a waist coat.
--	**Weather**	....	Atmospheric conditions.
	Whether	....	Which of the two alternative - I do not know whether they have arrived or not.
--	**Wave**	....	Swelling on the surface of water, to & fro in greeting or as a signal.
	Waive	....	No to insist on (a right, claim, opportunity) to relinquish.
--	**Whither**	....	To what / which place, position.
	Wither	....	To decay, to lose freshness, in a shrinking manner.
--	**Weight**	....	What is your weight?
	Wait	....	Wait a minute.
--	**Wander**	....	Do not wander above.
	Wonder	....	I wondered at his progress.
--	**Wine**	....	Wine is harmful to health.
	Vine	....	Grapes are hanging on vine.
--	**Wreath**	....	Flowers arranged in a circle, ring or curl of smoke or cloud.
	Wreathe	....	To twist, encircle as.
--	**Weak**	....	Deficient in strength, not strong.
	Week	....	Seven days
	Wick	....	Strip of thread in a lamp or candle.

--	**Yoke**	....	Frame or bar or dominion.
	Yolk	....	The yellow part of an egg (the yolk of an egg is a perfect food)
--	**Zealous**	....	One who works with zeal, ardent enthusiastic.
	Jealous	....	Envious, Suspicious.

****

Legal words

Common legal words, meaning/definition and its outlines.

LEGAL WORDS WITH DEFINITION

All the shorthand learners/high speed aspirants may also note that the following legal words are commonly used in all the matters / cases of the Hon'ble Courts. So, to avoid any awkward position to be faced while taking the dictation on legal matters by the learners/high speed aspirants, these words must be memorised / practised.

1.	**Applicant**	....	Anybody, who moved the application, may be the Plaintiff, Defendant or any other person.
2.	**Ad Interim Injunction**	....	Order by the Court thus restraining a person from doing a particular act for the time being during the pendency of the case.
3.	**Appeal**	....	When any application is moved in the Higher Court by the aggrieved party against an order.
4.	**Appellant**	....	A person who prefers an appeal.
5.	**A.P.P. (Addl.PP)**	....	Addl. Public Prosecutor - standing counsel for the Government representing it for criminal cases.
6.	**Accused**	....	A person facing the trial in the Court for the offences complained of against him.
7.	**Abatementum**	....	An entry upon land by way of interposition between the death of the ancestor and the entry of the heir.
8.	**Abatement**	....	Instigate to commit crime.
9.	**Abdication**	....	To renounce a post of office formerly or by default.

10.	**Abduction**	....	The offence of taking over a wife, child, ward or any Party by fraud and persuasion or open violence.
11.	**Abeyance**	....	Temporary suspension.
12.	**Adjuration**	....	Renunciation under oath, to renounce, abondon.
13.	**Absolve**	....	To set free.
14.	**Accompany**	....	To go along with.
15.	**Accredited Representative**	....	Representative having general authority to act.
16.	**Accrued Compensation**	....	Due and payable, but not yet paid.
17.	**Acquitted Acquittance**	....	Written discharge.
18.	**Adjournment**	....	To put off, postpone.
19.	**Adjudicate/tion**	....	To settle in the excercise of Judicial Authority.
20.	**Affirmative**	....	Confirming.
21.	**Aggravated/ Aggravation**	....	Assault with a dangerous weapon.
22.	**Alienate**	....	To convey, to transfer the title to property.
23.	**Ambiguity**	....	Doubtfulness.
24.	**Amicable Action**	....	An action carried on by the mutual consent.
25.	**Appellate Court (Appellator)**	....	A court having jurisdiction of appeal.
26.	**Arbitration/ Arbitrator**	....	Disputes solved by dis-interested person between two parties.

27.	Attorney General	....	Advocate who appears on behalf of Central Government.
28.	Breach of contract	....	If the person has not performed his contractual duties.
29.	Bankruptcy Proceeding	....	Action for bankruptcy under Court.
30.	Banevolence/ Banevolent	....	Purpose to do good to men.
31.	Borrower	....	Person who took a loan.
32.	Bail	....	An Order for releasing undertrial.
33.	Censorship	....	Board to do the work regarding editing news and pictures.
34.	Counsel	....	Advocate.
35.	Collateral	....	By the side, attached upon the side.
36.	Contempt	....	A willful dis-regard of a Public Authority.
37.	CPC	....or....	Code of Civil Procedure.
38.	Crl. P.C.	....	Code of Criminal Procedure.
39.	Charge	....	To make an accusation - thus apprising the person concerned of the offence complained of.
40.	Court Notice	....	It is issued by the Court, without any step by the party, in its own discretion.
41.	Case Property	....	The items connected with the case collected by the Police.
42.	Convict	....	A person who is held guilty by the Court for any offence.
43.	Defendant	....or....or....	A person against whom the suit is filed.

44.	**Demotion**	....	Degradation, putting to a lower grade/position.
45.	**Discrepancy**	....	Difference, dis-agreement.
46.	**Discretionary**	.... or	A power or right conferred upon one by law of acting as per his/her mind.
47.	**Dismissed in**	....	When the Plaintiff - who has filed the suit does not appear for pursuing the case, the suit is dismissed in default.
48.	**Dis-honour**	....	To refuse to accept to pay a cheque when duly presented.
49.	**Dismissal**	....	An order or judgement finally disposing of suit, an application.
50.	**Dispensation**	....	An exemption from some laws/ a relaxaltion of law for the benefit or advantage to an individual.
51.	**Disposition**	....	Transferring to the case or possession of another.
52.	**Dissolution**	....	Act or process of dissolving / termination.
53.	**Decree**	....	Final Order passed by the Court thus granting the relief sought by the Plaintiff in the suit.
54.	**Defence Evidence**	....	Evidence to be adduced by the accused in his defence.
55.	**Divorce**	....	Dissolution of marriage by order of the Court.
56.	**Dissolution of Marriage**	....	Order of the Court whereby the marriage between the Parties is dissolved.
57.	**Dasti**	....	Any order or paper ordered to be given by hand to the Party.

58.	**Dismiss**		When the Petition filed by the Party fails and is ordered as such by the Court.
59.	**Endowment**		Transfer generally as a gift, money or property to an institution for a particular purpose.
60.	**Enrolled Bill**		The final copy of a Bill or Joint resolution passed by both the Houses of Parliament/Legislature and ready for signature to become law.
61.	**Eviction**		Dis-possession by process of law.
62.	**Extinguishment**		Cancellation of a Right, Power.
63.	**Eye-witness**		A person who could testify as to what he had seen.
64.	**ex-Parte**		When the Defendant does not turn up on the date of hearing - one Side hearing in favour of Plaintiff/Petitioner.
65.	**Executory Agreement**		Such agreements as are to be performed in the future.
66.	**Fugitive**		One who flees, used in criminal law with the implication of a flight evasion or escape from arrest, imprisonment.
67.	**Interim Injunction**		Order by the Court restraining a person from doing a particular apt for the time being during the pendency of the case. It may also be a discretion to do an act.
68.	**Injunction**		Order by the court thus restraining a person from doing a particular act.
69.	**Issues**		The questions or points in dispute between the parties.

70.	**I.P.C.**	Indian Penal Code.
71.	**Illegal**	Not authorised by law.
72.	**Immaterial**	Not material, not necessary.
73.	**Immigration**	The formalities for coming into a country of a foreigners for purpose of temporary/permanent residence.
74.	**Infringement**	A breaking into, a tresspass or encroachment upon, a violation of a law / regulation.
75.	**Judicial Custody**	A person lying in the judicial custody of the Jail Authorities or sent to jail by the Order of the Court.
76.	**Judgement**	Final Order whicn is passed by disposing of the suit - case on merits.
77.	**Legislative**	To the process of enactment of laws.
78.	**Lessee**	One who rents property from another/purchaser.
79.	**Lessor**	One who rents property to another/seller.
80.	**Levy**	To assess, raise, the obtaining of money by the Government.
81.	**Litigation Express**	Amount to be paid by either Party towards contesting the case as advocate fee etc. and other miscellaneous expenses.
82.	**Legal Heirs**	A person who inherit assets & liabilities of the deceased.
83.	**Magistrate**	Public Civil Officer vested with executive or judicial powers.

84.	**Magisterial**	Relating to the character, office powers or duties of a Magistrate Or of the Magistracy.
85.	**Mandatory Injunction**	Command - order issued by the court for directing person to do a particular act.
86.	**M.C.A.**	Miscellaneous Civil Appeal - an appeal preferred against an order passed in between/during the pendency of the suit.
87.	**Maintenance Pendentelite**	Amount paid by the husband to the wife during the pendency of the case for her subsistance.
88.	**Non Applicant**	A person who is not a party to the application as an applicant.
89.	**Note**	Summon is always issued of the suit and notice is issued of the application filed by either party.
90.	**Order**	Every effective proceeding made during the continuation of the case.
91.	**Plaintiff**	A person who files the Suit/Plaint/Case.
92.	**Prosecute**	To follow up, to carry on an action or other judicial proceeding, to proceed against a person for punishing him/her in connection with the criminal offence committed by him/her.
93.	**Proxy Counsel**	Advocate who is representing the case of the Party on behalf of main Counsel.

94.	**Preventive Injunction**	....	Order issued by the Court for restraining a person from doing a Particular act.
95.	**Pendente lite Interest**	....	Interest on the amount accruing during the pendency of the case.
96.	**Pleadings**	....	Various pleas or contentions raised by the Parties.
97.	**Prosecution Evidence**	....	Witnesses led/examined in favour of the case.
98.	**Prosecution**	....	Institution and continuation of the case may be civil or criminal.
99.	**Prosecutor**	....	A person representing the case on behalf of the State.
100.	**Proclaimed Offender (PO)**	....	Proclaimed Offender - a person who does not appear in the Court after being released on Bail and is ordered as such by the Order of the Court.
101.	**Police Custody**	....	A person in th custody of Police.
102.	**Petitioner**	....	A person who files a Petition which normally filed in Matrimonial, Rent and Arbitration matters.
103.	**Parole**	....	To release an accused for few days to perform some social duties.
104.	**Replication**	....	Reply on behalf of the Plaintiff to the written statement of the defendant.
105.	**Rejoinder**	....	Reply on behalf of the Plaintiff to the written statement of the defendent. **or** Reply of the applicant to any new point or plea raised by the respondent in the reply.

106.	**Reply**	....	Answer to the contentions raised in the application.
107.	**Restore**	....	When a suit is dismissed in default and the Plaintiff moves application and shows sufficient cause for non-appearance, the suit may be restored.
108.	**R.C.A.**	....	Regular Civil Appeal - an appeal which is preferred on final disposal of the case by the trial court.
109.	**Respondent**	....	A person against whom the Petition is filed.
110.	**Restitution of Conjugal Rights**	....	Restoration of Matrimonial relations by the Order of the Court.
111.	**Relief**	....	Prayer - request made by the Party in the application.
112.	**Surety**	....	A person who undertake to produce the accused in the Court and furnish a Bond to this effect.
113.	**Surety Bond**	....	A Bond executed by the Surety to produce the accused in the Court.
114.	**Suit**	....	Case.
115.	**Summons**	....	Notice of the suit to the opposite party issued by the Court on Process fee.
116.	**Stay**	....	The word which is commonly used for injunction.
117.	**Solicitor**	....	Chief Law Officer of City, Highest post for an advocate for the State.
118.	**Set aside**	....	When the order proceeding against any Party is recalled-cancelled and he/she is permitted to contest the suit.

119. T.C.R. .... Trial Court Record

120. Territorial Property .... The land and water over which the state has jurisdiction and control

121. Undertrial .... A person facing trial.

122. Written Statement .... This is para-wise reply to the contents of the suit/plaint by the defendant.

Foreign Words

Foreign Words/Phrases, its proper meaning with outlines.

FOREIGN WORDS / PHRASES

It is well aware that now-a-days we use many foreign words and phrases in English language. In this chapter, we are giving a list of foreign words and phrases which are commonly used in the Shorthand Passages related to Legal matters, Reports of various Commissions & Committees and Parliamentary Speech also.

All the shorthand Learners/high speed aspirants should read these foreign words / phrases carefully and try to remember them with accurate outlines so that you can use them properly while transcribe your Shorthand passages.

Abbreviations are used in the following manner: **L** = Latin; **F** = French; **Sp.** = Spanish; **G** = Greek; **Gr** = German; **it** = Italian.

- **A bas (F)** .... Down with
- **Ab ante (L)** .... From before
- **Ab extra (L)** .... From without
- **Ab initio (L)** .... or .... From the beginning
- **Ab intra (L)** .... From within
- **Ab origine (L)** .... From the origin
- **Ab ovo (L)** .... From the beginning, from the egg.
- **A bras ouverts (F)** .... With arms wide open
- **Absit invidia (L)** .... Let there be no envy or ill feeling.
- **Addenda (L)** .... or .... Things to be added
- **Ad finem (L)** .... To the end
- **Ad hoc (L)** .... For a special purpose, for that special aim
- **A discretion (Fr.)** .... Without restriction

- **Adieu** .... Word of farewell spoken before a long or final parting.
- **A die (L)** .... From that day.
- **Ad extra (L)** .... Outward
- **Ad modum** .... After the method of.
- **Ad infinitum (L)** .... Without end or limit, indefinitely.
- **Ad interim (L)** .... In the meantime, in the meanwhile.
- **Ad libitum (L)** .... As one wishes , to the extent that one wishes.
- **Ad nauseam (L)** .... To the point of nausea, to satiety.
- **Ad referendum (L)** .... To be considered further, for further consideration.
- **Ad rem** .... Relevant, To the point.
- **Adsum (L)** .... I am present; Here.
- **Ad unguem (L)** .... To the nail; To a nicety; Exactly; Perfectly.
- **Ad valorem (L)** .... or .... According to him, according to value
- **Affaire d'amour (F)** .... A love affairs.
- **Affaire de coeur (F)** .... Love affair, matter concerning the feelings.
- **Affaire d'honneur (F)** .... An affair of honour.
- **A fond (Fr.)** .... Thoroughly
- **A fortiori (L)** .... With stronger reason.

- **Agent provocateur (F)** — Person deliberately stirring up unrest.
- **A huis clos (F)** — Privately, Secretly.
- **Aide (F)** — Helper, Assistant.
- **Aide memoire** — Notes to aid memory.
- **A la carte (F)** — Picking from the bill of fare.
- **A la mode (F)** — Fashionable, Up-to-date.
- **Alfresco (L)** — In the fresh or cool air.
- **Alias (L)** — Otherwise known as, generally indicating a variation of name
- **Alibi (L)** — Elsewhere.
- **Alma Mater (L)** — One's school or University.
- **Alter ego (L)** — One's other self, Person with whom one has much in common or who is one's inseparable companion.
- **Ame damnee (F)** — Person fated to bring about another's downfall.
- **Amende honorable (F)** — Handsome reparation or apology.
- **A merveille (F)** — Wonderfully, Very Well.
- **Amor patriae (L)** — Patriotic fervour.
- **Amour-propre (F)** — Self-esteem, Vanity
- **Anno Christi (L)** — In the year of Christ.
- **Anno Domini (L)** — In or after the year of our Lord's death

	Phrase	Outline	Meaning
-	**Anno mundi (L)**	....	In the year of the world
-	**Annus mirabilis (L)**	....	A or the year of wonders.
-	**Ante meridiem (L)**	....	Before noon
-	**A point (F)**	....	Exactly right or ready.
-	**Apropos (F)**	....	To the point
-	**A quatre**	....	Four together
-	**Ariston metron (Gr)**	....	The golden mean, The middle course.
-	**A toute force (Fr.)**	....	By all means
-	**A toute prix (Fr.)**	....	At any price
-	**Au courant (F)**	....	Having the latest information, up-to-date in one's knowledge, fully informed.
-	**Audi alteram partem (L)**	....	Hear the other side.
-	**Au fait (F)**	....	Well acquainted
-	**Auf wieder-sehen (Gr)**	....	Words of farewell spoken at a temporary separation.
-	**Au pis aller (F)**	....	If the worst should happen.
-	**Au revoir (F)**	....	Words of farewell spoken at a temporary separation.
-	**Aut vincere aut mori (L.)**	....	Death or victory, Do or die.
-	**Beau geste (F)**	....	Fine or noble gesture or action.
-	**Beau ideal (F)**	....	Ideal excellence, Imagined state of perfection.

-	**Beau monde (F)**	....	Fashionable society.
-	**Beaux yeux (F)**	....	Fine eyes, Beauty.
-	**Belles-letters (F)**	....	Literature that has aesthetic value.
-	**Ben trovato (It)**	....	Well said, Cleverly thought of.
-	**Bete noire (F)**	....	Bugbear, Black beast.
-	**Blunt und Elsen(Gr)**	....	Blood and iron (as means of gaining one's political ends).
-	**Bona fide (L)**	....	In good faith, Genuine
-	**Bon ami (F)**	....	Good friend
-	**Bon gre mal gre (F)**	....	Willy-nilly.
-	**Bonhomie (F)**	....	Good nature, Jovial manner
-	**Bonjour**	....	Good-morning, Good-day.
-	**Bon voyage (F)**	....	A good journey to you.
-	**Bourgeois (F)**	....	Middle class.
-	**Borne (Fr.)**	....	Narrow minded
-	**Cadre (Fr.)**	....	List of officers, a scheme.
-	**Canaille (F)**	....	Common people, Rabble
-	**Carte blanche (F)**	....	Blanket permission to do or spend as one pleases
-	**Cas d'urgence (F)**	....	Emergency.
-	**Casus belli (L)**	....	That which is at stake in a war.
-	**Causa sine quanon (L)**	....	An indispensable cause or condition.

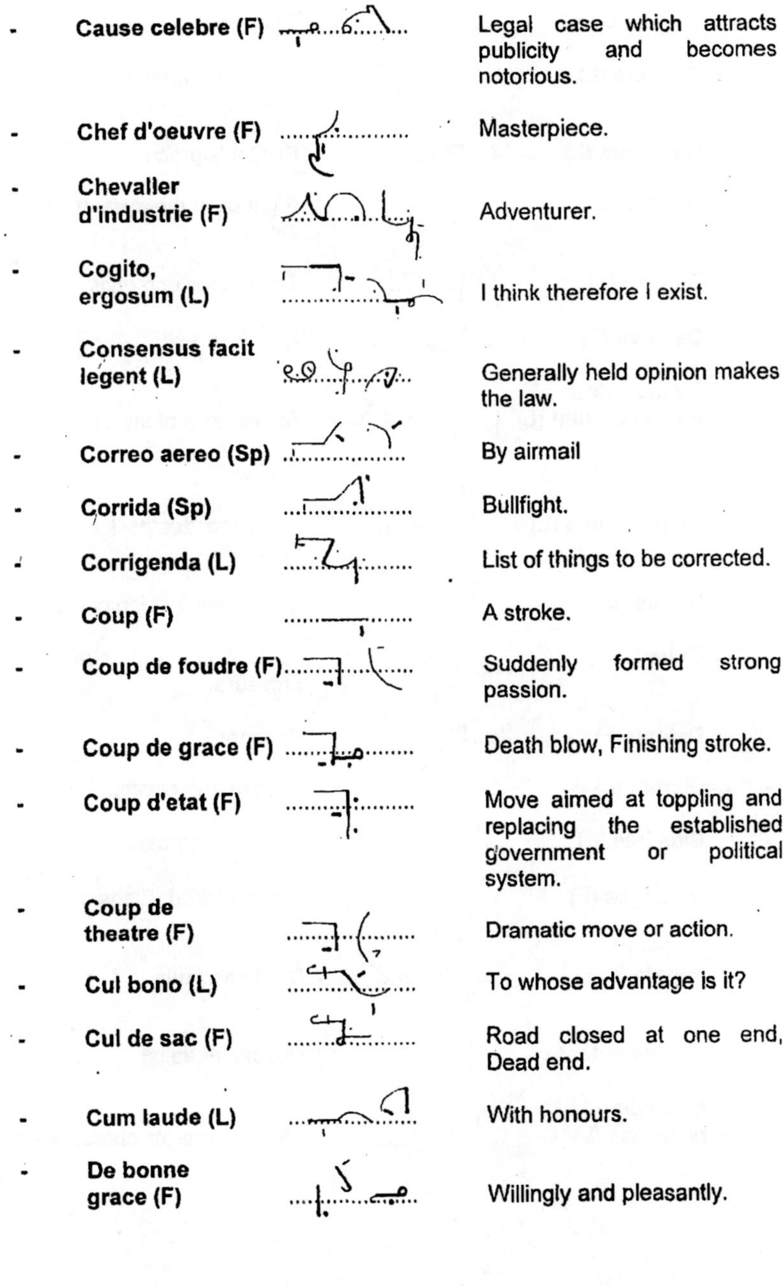

Cause celebre (F)	Legal case which attracts publicity and becomes notorious.
Chef d'oeuvre (F)	Masterpiece.
Chevaller d'industrie (F)	Adventurer.
Cogito, ergosum (L)	I think therefore I exist.
Consensus facit legent (L)	Generally held opinion makes the law.
Correo aereo (Sp)	By airmail
Corrida (Sp)	Bullfight.
Corrigenda (L)	List of things to be corrected.
Coup (F)	A stroke.
Coup de foudre (F)	Suddenly formed strong passion.
Coup de grace (F)	Death blow, Finishing stroke.
Coup d'etat (F)	Move aimed at toppling and replacing the established government or political system.
Coup de theatre (F)	Dramatic move or action.
Cul bono (L)	To whose advantage is it?
Cul de sac (F)	Road closed at one end, Dead end.
Cum laude (L)	With honours.
De bonne grace (F)	Willingly and pleasantly.

- **Da Capo (It.)** — From the beginning
- **De facto (L)** — Actual, by virtue of possession of fact
- **Dei gratia (L)** — By God's grace.
- **De jure (L)** — Rightful, in the eyes of the law
- **De luxe (F)** — The source and origin.
- **De novo (L)** — A new, afresh
- **De mortuis nil nisi bonum (L)** — Speak no ill of the dead.
- **Deo volente (L)** — God willing.
- **De profundis (L)** — From the depths (of sorrow etc.)
- **Dernier cri (F)** — Very latest fashion or craze.
- **Detente (F)** — Relaxation of strain or pressure.
- **Detenu (F)** — Prisoner
- **Dictum (L)** — Judgement, saying.
- **Dies irae (L)** — Day of judgement.
- **Distingue (F)** — Distinguished, Elegant
- **Divide et impera (L)** — Divide and rule.
- **Double entente** — Double meaning
- **Dramatis personae (L)** — The persons or characters in a drama.

- **Dum spiro spero(L)** .... While I breathe I hope, while there is life there is hope.
- **Elan (F)** .... Surge of feeling, Verve, Vivacity.
- **El Dorado (Sp)** .... The imaginary Golden Land (in South America)
- **Emeritus (L)** .... Retired from office.
- **En ami (F)** .... As a friend
- **En bloc (F)** .... As a whole, wholesale
- **En famille** .... As a family, among the members of a family
- **Enfant terrible (F)** .... Literally, a terrible child
- **En fete (F)** .... On holiday, in a state of festivity.
- **En masse (F)** .... All together, considered as Group, in a body
- **En rapport (F)** .... In harmony, in accordance, in touch.
- **En regle (F)** .... In due form, conforming to regulations.
- **En route (F)** .... On the way.
- **Entente cordiale(F)** .... Friendly agreement between States.
- **Entourage (F)** .... Surroundings; Adjuncts.
- **Entre nous (F)** .... Between ourselves, Privately.
- **Errata (L)** .... Errors.
- **Erratum (L)** .... Error.
- **Esprit de corps (F)** .... Team spirit, Regard for and sense of being part of a corporate body to which one belongs.

- **Et cetera (L)** .... And the rest
- **Et tu, Brute (L)** .... You too, Brutus (said to a friend who has betayed one).
- **Eureka (Gr.)** .... I have found it
- **Ex curia (L)** .... Out of court
- **Exempli gratia (L)** .... For example.
- **Ex gratia (L)** .... As an act of grace
- **Exhit (L)** .... Goes out
- **Exit (L)** .... The way out
- **Ex nihilo nihil fit (L)** .... Nothing comes of nothing
- **Ex officio (L)** .... By virtue of office or position
- **Ex Parte (L)** .... From or on behalf of one side only
- **Ex post facto (L)** .... Retrospective
- **Extempore (L)** .... Without previous preparation.
- **Elegant (Fr.)** .... A man of fashion
- **Ex voto (L)** .... According to one's prayer
- **Faire bonne mine (F)** .... Appear to be pleased.
- **Fait accompli (F)** .... A thing already done, completed action or deed.
- **Faux pas (F)** .... Blunder, tactless words or action.

-	**Fiat lux (L)**		Let there be light.
-	**Finis**		The end.
-	**Gendarme (F)**	or	A body of armed police in France.
-	**Gourmand (F)**		One who enjoys eating.
-	**Gourmet (F)**		One who enjoys eating good, well prepared food.
-	**Hoch (Gr)**		Your health.
-	**Hoi polloi (G)**		The common people.
-	**Hominis est errare(L)**		It is human to err.
-	**Hors de combat (F)**		Unfit to fight, not in the running.
-	**Hors d'oeuvre (F)**		LIght first dish served as an appetizer for a meal.
-	**Ibidem (L)**		In the same place.
-	**Idee fixe (F)**		Dominating idea that will not be banished, obsession.
-	**Idem (L)**		The same.
-	**Idest (L)**		That is.
-	**Ignorantia (L)**		Ignorance of the point under discussion.
-	**Impasse (F)**		A dead end, An insoluble difficulty.
-	**Impedimenta (L)**		Baggage.
-	**In camera (L)**		In a (Judge's Private Room)
-	**In curia (L)**		In Court

- **In extenso (L)** .... At full length
- **Infra dig (L)** .... Below one's position.
- **In memoriam (L)** .... To the memory of
- **In re (L)** .... In the matter of
- **In sano sensu (L)** .... In proper sense.
- **In situ (L)** .... In its original situation
- **Inter nos (L)** .... Between ourselves
- **Inter alia (L)** .... Among other things
- **Inter se (L)** .... Amongst themselves
- **In toto (L)** .... In the whole, entirely
- **Ipso facto** .... Really, by this very fact
- **Ipso jure (L)** .... By the law itself
- **In vino veritas (L)** .... Truth lies in wine, one speaks the truth when drunk.
- **Jure Divino (L)** .... By divine law.
- **Jus civile (L)** .... The civil law
- **Jus divinum (L)** .... The divine law.
- **Jus gentium (L)** .... Law between nations.
- **Lacta alea est (L)** .... The die is cast, an irreversible decision has been taken.
- **Laissez faire** .... A policy of non-interference deliberate non-intervention
- **Laus Deo (L)** .... Praise to God.
- **Lingua franca (L)** .... A common language.

- **Locus standi (L)** .... Recognised position right to interfere
- **Ma chere (F)** .... My dear (fem.)
- **Magnum Opus (L)** .... Great work.
- **Mal a propos (F)** .... Badly timed, Inapposite.
- **Mala fide (L)** .... Faithlessly, with bad faith
- **Mandamus (L)** .... An order issued by a High Court requiring an inferior court or a corporation to do something which pertains to its office.
- **Mariage de convenance (F)** .... Marriage arranged to promote financial interests, marriage for money and not for love.
- **Matinee (F)** .... A public entertainment held in afternoon
- **Mea culpa (L)** .... The fault is mine.
- **Me judice (L)** .... I being judge; In my opinion, in my opinion as a judge.
- **Mesalliance (F)** .... Marriage with someone of lower social status.
- **Modus Operandi (L)** .... Method of working or functioning, mode of operating.
- **Modus vivendi (L)** .... Way of life, Temporary arrangement of harmony or co-operation pending a final settlement.
- **Mon ami (F)** .... My friend.

- **More suo (L)** .... In his own way.
- **Mutatis Mutandis (L)** .... With the necessary changes having been made.
- **Nee (F)** .... Born, Her maiden name being.
- **Ne plus ultra (L)** .... That which is unsurpassable, Perfection, nothing further.
- **Nihil ad rem (L)** .... Nothing to the point.
- **Nil desperandum** .... There is no reason for despair.
- **N'importe (F)** .... It matters not, it does not matter.
- **Nom blesse oblige (F)** .... Elevated rank entails obligations.
- **Nom de plume (F)** .... Assumed name used by an author when writing.
- **Nota bene (L)** .... Mark well, take notice
- **Nouveau riche (F)** .... One newly enriched
- **Nudis verbis (L)** .... In plain words.
- **Obiter dictum (dicta)(L)** .... Casual remark, Opinion given by a judge incidentally and not having binding force.
- **Observanda (L)** .... Things to be observed
- **Par exemple (Fr.)** .... For example
- **Par avion (F)** .... By air mail.

	Term	Outline	Meaning
-	Par excellence (F)	....	Pre eminent, outstanding, eminently
-	Per (L)	....	For, through, by.
-	Peccavi (L)	....	I have sinned.
-	Per annum (L)	.... or	A year, by the year, per year
-	Per capita (L)	....	Per head
-	Per diem (L)	....	Per day, daily
-	Per mensem (L)	....	Per month.
-	Per se (L)	....	In itself, Considered in isolation.
-	Persona grata (L)	....	A person who is held in special favour.
-	Persona non grata (L)	....	Unwelcome person, Person unwillingly received.
-	Per centum (L)	....	By the hundred, per hundred.
-	Personnel (Fr.)	....	Persons employed in any service or business
-	Piece de resistance (F)	....	Most spectacular item, Greatest achievement.
-	Post meridiem P.M. (L)	....	Afternoon
-	Prescriptum (L)	....	Things prescribed
-	Prima facie (L)	....	On first consideration, On the first view
-	Primo (L)	....	In the first place.

- **Primus inter pares (L)** — Ranking first among equals.
- **Pro bono publico (L)** — For public good.
- **Pro forma (L)** — For the sake of form, according to the form
- **Pro patria (It)** — For one's country
- **Pro rata (L)** — In proportion
- **Protege (F)** — Dependent, Patronised by others.
- **Pro tempore (It)** — For the time being.
- **Quantum (L)** — Quantity or amount
- **Quantum sufficit (L)** — A sufficient quantity
- **Quid pro quo (L)** — Something in return: An equivalent.
- **Qui tacet consentit (L)** — Silence means consent.
- **Quod erat faciendum** — Which was to be done.
- **Qui vive (F)** — Who goes there?
- **Raison d'etat (F)** — A reason of state.
- **Raison d'etre (F)** — Reason for existing, basic justification.
- **Rapprochment (F)** — Increase in cordiality or intimacy.
- **Re (L)** — With regard to, in the matter of.

-	**Resume (F)**	....	Summary or Abstract
-	**Sic (L)**	....	Thus, often used to call attention to some quoted mistake.
-	**Sine cura (L)**	....	Without charge or care.
-	**Sine die (L)**	....	Without a definite day, of a meeting adjourned for an indefinite period
-	**Sine dubio (L)**	....	Without the slightest doubt.
-	**Sine qua non (L)**	....	An indispensable condition.
-	**Soiree (F)**	....	Evening party.
-	**Status quo (L)**	....	The state in which the pre-existing state of affairs, the state or condition in which a thing is existing.
-	**Statu quo ante bellum (L)**	....	In the state in which things were before the war.
-	**Stet (L)**	....	Let it stand.
-	**Sub judice (L)**	.... or	Under consideration
-	**Sub rosa (L)**	....	Under the rose, Secretly.
-	**Sub poena (L)**	.... or	Under a penalty.
-	**Sui juris (L)**	....	In one's own right.
-	**Summum bonum (L)**	....	The chief good.
-	**Sanctum Sanctorum (L)**	....	Holy of holies, Inner sanctuary.

- **Tabula rasa (L)** .... Complete blank, Surface ready to be written on.
- **Te judice (F)** .... You being the judge.
- **Tempus fugit (L)** .... Time flies.
- **Terra Incognita (L)** .... Unknown land, unexplored territory.
- **Tete-a-tete (F)** .... Intimate or private converstation between two people.
- **Tiers etat (F)** .... The third estates, The common people.
- **Tour de force (F)** .... Skilful achievement, Stroke of genius.
- **Ubique (L)** .... Everywhere
- **Ultra vires (L)** .... Beyond one's powers
- **Ultima ratio (L)** .... Final argument.
- **Veni, vidi, vici (L)** .... I came, I saw, I conquered
- **Verbatim et litteratim (L)** .... Word for word and letter for letter.
- **Versus (L)** .... Against
- **Via (L)** .... By way of
- **Vice (L)** .... In the place of
- **Via - media (L)** .... The middle course
- **Vice - versa (L)** .... The other way round, the order being reversed
- **Vide (L)** .... See.

-	**Vis-a-vis (Fr.)**	....	With regard to, towards, facing, opposite.
-	**Viva-voce**	....	By oral testimony, orally
-	**Viz**	....	Namely
-	**Vox populi (L)**	....	The voice of the people.
-	**Volte face (L)**	....	A change of front.
-	**Vulgo (L)**	....	Commonly.
-	**Zeitgeist (Gr)**	....	The spirit of the times.

<u>Note</u> All the shorthand learners/high speed aspirants should practise the outlines of the foreign words/phrases attentively so as to avoid any mistakes whenever they transcribe their shorthand dictated passage

****

Form of Verbs

Form of Verbs with distinctive outlines for similar forms.

Form of Verbs

The knowledge of verbs is essential to the shorthand learners/high speed aspirants to achieve the targeted point efficiently. If the placing of outlines are the similar, then learners / high speed aspirants may use the vowel indication to distinguish the same in the following manner.

The form of verbs are given below with outlines-

Present	Past	Past Participle	Outline
Abide	Abode	Abode	....
Arise	Arose	Arisen	....
Awake	Awoke, Awaked	Awoke, Awaked	....
Awaken	Awakened	Awakened	....
Am	Was	Been	....
Act	Acted	Acted	....
Advise	Advised	Advised	....
Abuse	Abused	Abused	....
Ask	Asked	Asked	....
Accuse	Accused	Accused	....
Allow	Allowed	Allowed	....
Answer	Answered	Answered	....
Appear	Appeared	Appeared	....
Attack	Attacked	Attacked	....
Arrive	Arrived	Arrived	....
Arrest	Arrested	Arrested	....

Appoint	Appointed	Appointed	
Argue	Argued	Argued	
Buy	Bought	Bought	
Beg	Begged	Begged	
Bend	Bent	Bent	
Bring	Brought	Brought	
Burn	Burnt	Burnt	
Boil	Boiled	Boiled	
Build	Built	Built	
Beat	Beat	Beaten	
Become	Became	Become	
Blow	Blew	Blown	
Break	Broke	Broken	
Bind	Bound	Bound	
Bear	Bore	Bore	
Bid	Bade, Bid	Bidden, Bid	
Bathe	Bathed	Bathed	
Borrow	Borrowed	Borrowed	
Boast	Boasted	Boasted	
Believe	Believed	Believed	
Beget	Begot	Begotten	
Begin	Began	Begun	

Behold	Beheld	Beheld	....
Bereave	Bereaved	Bereaved	....
Beseech	Besought	Besought	....
Bite	Bit	Bit, Bitten	....
Bleed	Bled	Bled	....
Blend	Blended	Blended	....
Breed	Bred	Bred	....
Burst	Burst	Burst	....
Cast	Cast	Cast	....
Catch	Caught	Caught	....
Chide	Chid	Chidden, Child	....
Choose	Chose	Chosen	....
Cleave	Cleft, Clove	Cleft, Cloven	....
Cling	Clung	Clung	....
Come	Came	Come	....
Cost	Cost	Cost	....
Creep	Crept	Crept	....
Crow	Crowed, Crew	Crowed	....
Cut	Cut	Cut	....
Can	Could	Could	....
Clothe	Clothed, Clad	Clothed, Clad	....
Call	Called	Called	....

Carry	Carried	Carried	
Copy	Copied	Copied	
Care	Cared	Cared	
Clean	Cleaned	Cleaned	
Change	Changed	Changed	
Collect	Collected	Collected	
Climb	Climbed	Climbed	
Cook	Cooked	Cooked	
Close	Closed	Closed	
Cross	Crossed	Crossed	
Cry	Cried	Cried	
Count	Counted	Counted	
Clear	Cleared	Cleared	
Consult	Consulted	Consulted	
Dare	Dared	Dared	
Deal	Dealt	Dealt	
Do	Did	Done	
Draw	Drew	Drawn	
Dream	Dreamt, Dreamed	Dreamt, Dreamed	
Drive	Drove	Driven	
Dwell	Dwelt/Dwelled	Dwelt/Dwelled	
Die	Died	Died	

Dig	Dug	Dug	....
Dip	Dipped	Dipped	....
Drink	Drank	Drunk	....
Drown	Drowned	Drowned	....
Dye	Dyed	Dyed	....
Defeat	Defeated	Defeated	....
Dry	Dried	Dried	....
Deliver	Delivered	Delivered	....
Eat	Ate	Eaten	....
Earn	Earned	Earned	....
Enter	Entered	Entered	....
End	Ended	Ended	....
Ebb	Ebbed	Ebbed	....
Economise	Economised	Economised	....
Echo	Echoed	Echoed	....
Edify	Edified	Edified	....
Evade	Evaded	Evaded	....
Evoke	Evoked	Evoked	....
Fall	Fell	Fallen	....
Feed	Fed	Fed	....
Feel	Felt	Felt	....
Fell	Felled	Felled	....

Fight	Fought	Fought	
Find	Found	Found	
Flee	Fled	Fled	
Fling	Flung	Flung	
Fly	Flew	Flown	
Forbear	Forbore	Forborne	
Forbid	Forbad	Forbidden	
Forget	Forgot	Forgot, Forgotten	
Forgive	Forgave	Forgiven	
Forsake	Forsook	Forsaken	
Freeze	Froze	Frozen	
Get	Got	Got	
Gild	Gilt, Gilded	Gilt, Gilded	
Give	Gave	Given	
Go	Went	Gone	
Grind	Ground	Ground	
Grow	Grew	Grown	
Gird	Girt, Girded	Girt, Girded	
Hang	Hung, Hanged	Hung, Hanged	
Have	Had	Had	
Hear	Heard	Heard	
Heave	Heaved	Heaved	

Hew	Hewed	Hewn, Hewed	
Hide	Hid	Hidden	
Hit	Hit	Hit	
Hold	Held	Held	
Hurt	Hurt	Hurt	
Keep	Kept	Kept	
Knit	Knit, Knitted	Knit, Knitted	
Kneel	Knelt/Kneeled	Knelt/Kneeled	
Know	Knew	Known	
Lay	Laid	Laid	
Lead	Led	Led	
Leap	Leapt, Leaped	Leapt, Leaped	
Learn	Learnt, Learned	Learnt, Learned	
Leave	Left	Left	
Lend	Lent	Lent	
Let	Let	Let	
Lie	Lay	Lain	
Lie	Lied	Lied	
Light	Lighted, Lit	Lighted, Lit	
Lose	Lost	Lost	
Make	Made	Made	
Mean	Meant	Meant	

Melt	Melted	Melted	
May	Might	Might	
Owe	Owed	Owed	
Pen	Penned	Penned	
Put	Put	Put	
Quit	Quit	Quit	
Raise	Raised	Raised	
Read	Read	Read	
Rent	Rent	Rent	
Ride	Rode	Ridden	
Ring	Rang	Rung	
Rise	Rose	Risen	
Rot	Rotted	Rotted, Rotten	
Run	Ran	Run	
Saw	Sawed	Sawn, Sawed	
Say	Said	Said	
See	Saw	Seen	
Seek	Sought	Sought	
Sell	Sold	Sold	
Send	Sent	Sent	
Sew	Sewed	Sewn, Sewed	
Shake	Shook	Shaken	

Shave	Shaved	Shaved	
Shear	Sheared	Shorn	
Shed	Shed	Shed	
Shine	Shone	Shone	
Shoot	Shot	Shot	
Show	Showed	Shown	
Shrink	Shrank	Shrunk	
Shut	Shut	Shut	
Sing	Sang	Sung	
Sink	Sank	Sunk	
Sleep	Slept	Slept	
Slide	Slid	Slid	
Smell	Smelt	Smelt	
Smite	Smote	Smitten	
Sow	Sowed	Sown, Sowed	
Speak	Spoke	Spoken	
Speed	Sped	Sped	
Spell	Spelled, Spelt	Spelled, Spelt	
Spend	Spent	Spent	
Spill	Spilt, Spilled	Spilt, Spilled	
Spin	Span	Spun	
Spit	Spat, Spit	Spat, Spit	

Split	Split	Split	....
Spoil	Spoiled, Spoilt	Spoiled, Spoilt	....
Spread	Spread	Spread	....
Spring	Sprang	Sprung	....
Stand	Stood	Stood	....
Steal	Stole	Stolen	....
Stick	Stuck	Stuck	....
Sting	Stang	Stang	....
Strew	Strewed	Strewn	....
Stride	Strode	Stridden, Strode	....
Strike	Struck	Struck	....
String	Strung	Strung	....
Strive	Strove	Striven	....
Swear	Swore	Sworn	....
Sweep	Swept	Swept	....
Swell	Swelled	Swelled, Swoller	....
Swim	Swam	Swum	....
Swing	Swang	Swung	....
Shall	Should	Should	....
Take	Took	Taken	....
Take	Taught	Taught	....
Thrive	Thrived, Throve	Thriven	....

Throw	Threw	Thrown	....
Thrusf	Thrust	Thrust	....
Tread	Trod	Trodden, Trod	....
Understand	Understood	Understood	....
Wake	Woke, Waked	Woken, Waked	....
Wash	Washed	Washed	....
Wear	Wore	Worn	....
Wed	Wed, Wedded	Wed, Wedded	....
Weep	Wept	Wept	....
Win	Won	Won	....
Work	Worked	Worked	....
Wish	Wished	Wished	....
Wring	Wrung	Wrung	....
Write	Wrote	Written	....
Weave	Wove	Woven	....
Will	Would	Would	....
Wind	Wound	Wound	....

****

Preposition

Preposition, its proper use with outlines.

PREPOSITION

A preposition is a part of speech which is used to show the relation of one noun or pronoun to another in a sentence, and is usually placed before the word which expresses the object of the relation. The use of preposition is largely governed by the usage of English. A change in preposition may change the whole meaning of the phrase or the sentence. Therefore, a knowledge of the correct use of preposition is essentially required for the shorthand learners/high speed aspirants.

So, all the shorthand learners/high speed aspirants may read the following words and its preposition carefully and try to remember them so that they can use it perfectly while transcribe the dictated passage to avoid such type of common mistakes.

	Words	Prepositions	Outlines
-	Abatement	Of	....
-	Abhorrence	Of	....
-	Ability	For	....
-	Absence	From	....
-	Abstinence	From	....
-	Abundance	Of	....
-	Abide	By	....
-	Abounds	In	....
-	Abstain	From	....
-	Absorbed	In	....
-	Access	To	....
-	Act	Upon	....
-	Accede	To	....
-	Account	For	....

-	Accused	Of	....
-	Accomplished	In	....
-	Accustomed	To	....
-	Accompanied	By	....
-	Acquit	Of	....
-	Acquaint	With	....
-	Acquaintance	With	....
-	Accomplice	With	....
-	(In) Accordance	With	....
-	Adapted	To, For, From	....
-	Agree	To, With, On, Upon	....
-	Adherence	To	....
-	Admission	To (a person)	
	Admission	Into (a piece)	....
-	Admiration	Of	....
-	Advantage	Of (his presence)	
	Advantage	Over (a person)	....
-	Addict	To	....
-	Adopt	To	....
-	Adequate	To	....
-	Adjacent	To	....
-	Admit	To, Into, Of	....
-	Affection	For	....
-	Affectionate	To	....
-	Afraid	Of	....

- Affinity	With	....
- Aim	At	....
- Alarmed	At	....
- Alive	To, With	....
- Allot	To	....
- Alight	From	....
- Allegiance	To	....
- Alliance	With	....
- Allusion	To	....
- Alternative	To	.... or
- Ambition	For	....
- Amazed	At	....
- Amused	With	....
- Angry	With, At	....
- Annoyed	At	.... or
- Anxious	For	....
- Answerable	To	....
- Analogy	Of	....
- Antidote	To	....
- Anxiety	For	....
- Antipathy	To	....
- Appeal	To	....
- Apprehension	Of	....
- Apologise	To	....

-	Applicable	To	....
-	Appoint	To	....
-	Appointment	With	....
-	Approve	Of	....
-	Aptitude	For	....
-	Apply	For, To	....
-	Arrive	At, In	....
-	Arrival	At, In	....
-	Assent	To	....
-	Ashamed	Of	....
-	Ask	For	....
-	Associate	With	....
-	Assurance, Assure	Of	....
-	Astonish	At	.... or
-	Attend	To, Upon	....
-	Attachment	To	....
-	Attention	To	....
-	Authority	Over	....
-	Avail	Of	....
-	Averse	To	....
-	Avenge	On	....
-	Aversion	To	....
-	Aware	Of	....
-	Award	To	....
-	Bark	At	....

	Word	Preposition	Outline
-	Bargain	With, For	
-	Benevolence	Towards	or
-	Betrayal	Of	
-	Become	Of	
-	Begged	Of, For	
-	Believe	In	
-	Belongs	To	
-	Benefit	By	
-	Beneficial	To	or
-	Bent	On	
-	Beset	With	
-	Beware	Of	
-	Blessed	With	
-	Blind	Of, To	
-	Boast	Of	
-	Bound	For	
-	Borrow	From	
-	Born	Of, To, In	
-	Break	Into, Down	
-	Brood	Over	
-	Buy	Of, From	
-	Busy	In, With	
-	Call	At, On	
-	Candidate	For	
-	Care	For	

-	Careful	About	....
-	Cause	Of, For	....
-	Capacity	For	....
-	Caution	Against	....
-	Certain	Of	....
-	Claim	On, To	....
-	Come	Across	....
-	Commit	To	....
-	Compare	With, To	....
-	Compete	With	....
-	Complain	To, Against, Of	....
-	Compassion	For	....
-	Compensation	For	....
-	Competition	With	....
-	Comply	With	....
-	Confident	Of	....
-	Congratulate	On	....
-	Connive	At	....
-	Conform	To	....
-	Confide	To, In	....
-	Consist	Of, In	....
-	Contrary	To	....
-	Control	Over	....

- Convict	Of	....
- Convince	Of	....
- Count	On, Upon	....
- Conscious	Of	....
- Correspond	With, To	....
- Conceal	From	....
- Cope	With	....
- Cruel	To	....
- Cure	Of, For	....
- Cling	To	....
- Commence	On	....
- Confer	On	....
- Crowned	With	....
- Courteous	To	....
- Deaf	To	....
- Deal	In, With	....
- Dear	To	....
- Demand	For	....
- Depend	On	....
- Dependent	On, For	....
- Deprive	Of	....
- Desire	For	....
- Desirous	Of	....
- Lesist	From	....

-	Despair	Of	....
-	Devoid	Of	....
-	Devote	To	....
-	Deficient	In	....
-	Derive	From	....
-	Deter	From	.... or
-	Dedicate	To	....
-	Die	Of, From	....
-	Differ	From, With	....
-	Disappointed	In	....
-	Disgrace	To	....
-	Dismiss	From	....
-	Dispense	With	....
-	Dispose	Of	....
-	Different	From	....
-	Disgusted	With	....
-	Displeased	With	....
-	Dissuade	From	....
-	Due	To	....
-	Duty	To	....
-	Dull	Of	....
-	Eager	For	....
-	Eat	Into	....
-	Eligible	For	....
-	Easy	Of	....

	Word	Preposition	
-	Elate	With	....
-	Employed	At, In, On, By, For	....
-	Endow	With	....
-	Engage	In, To	....
-	Enlist	In	....
-	Enquire	Of, Into, After	....
-	Enter	Upon, At	....
-	Entitle	To	....
-	Encroach	Upon, On	....
-	Entrust	To, With	....
-	Envious	Of	....
-	Enmity	With	....
-	Engrossed	In	....
-	Enrage	With	....
-	Enter	Upon, at	....
-	Equal	To	....
-	Essential	To	....
-	Escape	From	....
-	Esteem	For	....
-	Excel	In	....
-	Exception	To	....
-	Exchange	With	....
-	Excuse	For, From	....
-	Exempt	From	....
-	Expert	In	....

Expose	To	....
Exclude	From	....
Faithful	To	....
False	To	....
Familiar	With, To	....
Famous	For	....
Fatal	To	....
Favourable	For, To	....
Fail	In	....
Feed	On	....
Feel	For	....
Fight	With, Against, For	....
Fill	With	....
Fit	For	....
Followed	By	....
Fond	Of	....
Fondness	For	....
Forgetful	Of	....
Fortunate	In	....
Fraught	With	....
Free	From, To	....
Frown	At	....
Friendly	To	....
Furnish	With	....
Freedom	From, Of	....

-	Gifted	With
-	Glad	At, Of
-	Good	At, For, Of, To
-	Guilty	Of
-	Grateful	To, For
-	Gratitude	For, To
-	Grief	For, At
-	Greedy	Of
-	Grumble	At, About
-	Guard	Against
-	Hanker	After
-	Hard	Of
-	Hatred	For
-	Heard	Of
-	Heir	To
-	Hide	From
-	Hinder	From
-	Honest	In
-	Hope	For, Of
-	Hopeful	Of
-	Horrify	At
-	Hostile	To
-	Ignorant	Of
-	ill	With
-	Impose	On

- Impress On, Upon, With
- Import From
- Impertinent To
- Indebted To
- Indifferent To
- Indignant With, At .... or ....
- Inflict On
- Infest With
- Influence Over, With
- Inform Of
- Injurious To
- Inspire With
- Insist On
- Interference With
- Interest In
- Intimate With
- Introduce To
- Invite To
- Insensible To
- Indispensable To
- Involved In
- Indulgent To
- Irrelevant To
- Jealous Of
- Jeer At

	Word	Preposition	Outline
-	Jest	At	....
-	Join	To, In	....
-	Judge	Of	....
-	Jump	At, To	....
-	Junior	To, In, By	....
-	Key	To	....
-	Keen	About, On	....
-	Kind	To	....
-	Keep	To	....
-	Knock	At	....
-	Known	To	....
-	Lame	Of	....
-	Lament	For	....
-	Laugh	At	....
-	Lead	To	....
-	Lean	Against, On	....
-	Level	With, At	....
-	Liable	To	....
-	Liking	For	....
-	Limit	To	....
-	Listen	To	....
-	Live	On	....
-	Lost	To	....
-	Loyal	To	....
-	Long	For	....

- Look After
- Lust For
- Made Of
- Marry To, Into
- Match For
- Malice Against
- Mad With
- Marvel At
- Meddle With
- Meet With
- Mindful Of
- Mix With
- Mistake For
- Mourn For
- Move With
- Necessary For
- Need For, Of
- Neglectful Of
- Negligent In, Of
- Notorious For
- Obedient To
- Object To
- Objection To
- Obliged To
- Occupy With, In

	Word	Preposition
-	Occur	To
-	Offend	With
-	Opposed	To
-	Opportunity	For
-	Originate	In, With
-	Overwhelm	With
-	Part	From, With
-	Pay	For
-	Painful	To
-	Participate	In
-	Partial	To
-	Partnership	In
-	Passion	For
-	Perseverance	In
-	Peculiar	To
-	Perish	By, With
-	Persist	In
-	Pity	For
-	Pine	For
-	Play	On
-	Please	With, At
-	Pouring	Over
-	Popular	With
-	Power	Over
-	Pray	To

•	Prejudice	Against	
•	Preside	Over	
•	Prevail	On	
•	Prey	To, On	
•	Prefer	To	
•	Prevent	From	
•	Profit	By	
•	Protect	Against	
•	Proof	Of, Against	
•	Qualify	For	
•	Quarrel	With, Over	
•	Quick	Of, At	
•	Recommend	To	
•	Refer	To	
•	Regret	For	
•	Regard	For	
•	Relation	Of, To, Between	
•	Refrain	From	
•	Rejoice	At, In	
•	Rely	On	
•	Relieve	Of	
•	Remember	To	
•	Remind	Of	
•	Repent	Of	
•	Respect	For	

- Respectful To
- Responsible To
- Rest On, With
- Restore To
- Retire From
- Revenge On
- Remedy For
- Repentance For
- Reply To
- Reputation For
- Resemblance To
- Sacred To
- Satisfy With
- Save From
- Search For
- Seek For
- Send For
- Sensitive To
- Sentence To
- Share Of, With
- Shock At
- Short Of
- Showed Round
- Sin Against
- Sick Of

Similar	To	....
Slave	To	....
Sorry	For	....
Stare	At	....
Stay	At	....
Succeed	In, To	....
Submission	To	....
Subscription	To	....
Suspicion	Of	....
Supply	With, To	....
Sure	Of	....
Sympathise	With	....
Sympathy	For, To	....
Taste	For	....
Think	Of, Over	....
Tired	Of, With	....
Traitor	To	....
Traffic	In, With	....
Triumph	Over	....
True	To	.... or
Trust	In, With	....
Used	To	....
Useful	To	....
Vain	For, To	....

- Victory	Over	....
- Venture	Upon	....
- Vote	For	....
- Wait	For, On, At	....
- Withdraw	From	....
- Warn	Of, Against	....
- Welcome	To	....
- Wisn	For	....
- Wonder	At	....
- Worthy	Of	....
- Yield	Of	....
Yearn	For	....

****

Punctuation & Capital Letters

Proper use of punctuation marks and Capital Letters with some Un-punctuated/Punctuated passage.

Punctuation with Capital Letters

Punctuation is the art of indicating certain marks in order to make the meaning clearer of the shorthand passage dictated. However, the following points are always to be borne in mind by all the shorthand learners/high speed aspirants who wants to reach at the top in the field of Stenography as the punctuation is the art of using proper stops and marks so as to make the sense of a sentence or a shothand passage quite clear.

I. The Full Stop (.)
II. The Comma (,)
III. The Semicolon (;)
IV. The Colon (:)
V. The Sign of Interrogation (?)
VI. The Sign of Exclamation (!)
VII. The Inverted Commas (" ")
VIII. The Hyphen (-)
IX. The Dash (---)
X. The Apostrophe (')
XI. The Brackets ( )
XII. The CAPITAL LETTERS.

These stops or points are called the **"marks of punctuation"** and these should be memorised as it is well known that the wrong punctuation may sometimes alter the meaning of a sentence; a thorough knowledge of the fundamental rules covering the correct use of punctuation marks is indispensable to the shorthand writer, who wishes to transcribe the dictated passage by expressing the thoughts, ideas and feeling clearly, accurately and logically.

So, all the shorthand learners/high speed aspirants may always kept in mind all the rules/procedures of the punctuation marks. The following points of punctuation are, however, to be learnt attentively.

I. THE FULL STOP OR PERIOD (.)

The **Full Stop (.)** indicates the longest pause which is commonly be used.

1. At the end of every sentence other than Interrogative, Exclamatory and Optative; as

- She lost his pen and purse.
- This is the new site of our office.

2. Secondly, it is placed after abbreviations and no space is left between the two letters e.g.

- M.A., M.B.B.S., L.L.B., S.H.O. etc.

3. It is used at the end of an indirect question and not to be used after the direct question.

- Tell me what he said.
- I should like to know how you do it.

4. When the question is really a form of polite request.

- Will you please pass me the salad.
- Could I have a look at your watch, please.

5. After assertive and imperative sentence.

- The mother kissed her dear child. (Assertive)
- Do not mix with bad girls. (Imperative)
- Hang up your coat. (Imperative)

6. Always put the period / stop within quotation marks.

- I have ready "Leaves of Grass."
- He did not see the performance of "Mourning becomes Electra."

II. <u>THE COMMA</u> (,)

The function of the comma is to break up the sentence into separate thoughts in the interest of clarity and ease of reading. This mark of punctuation is used for shortest Pause in writing and speaking. However, it is used as under:-

1. **It separates two or more words of the same parts of Speech (generally nouns) where the last word is often separate by <u>and</u> or <u>or</u> ; as**

   - Vipin, Sanjeev and Rajesh are fast friends. (Proper Noun)
   - She is calm, wise, modest, truthful, diligent and intelligent. (Adjectives)
   - He bought books, registers, pencils and erasers. (Nouns)
   - She writes quickly, neatly and correctly. (Adverbs)
   - He laughed, sang, danced and made merry. (Verbs)

2. **It is used after the vocatives:-**

   - Ladies & Gentlemen, we are different but one countrymen.
   - Sir, I would like to talk about puctuality first.

3. **It is used to separate adverbs and adverbial phrases and Clauses:-**

   - First of all, this thing is going on the table.
   - Firstly, we want to see this boy in the first row.
   - Yes, he is known to me.
   - He, willingly or unwillingly, does everything to pass this exam.

4. **It separates date and the year:-**

   - July 7, 1997, our exam are starting in which 4000 candidates will have to show their performance.

5. **It is also used to separate two co-ordinate clauses:-**

   - I went, I saw him there.
   - She does it, she loves it.

6. **The most important use of Comma is its placement before and after the insertion of any sort in a sentence e.g.**

   - We want to, if the Government allows, form or forum.

- The Bill has laid emphasis, which we already have discussed, on many points.

7. To separate each pair of words connected by 'and' or 'or'; as,

- High and low, rich and poor, wise and foolish, all have to die.

8. Before and after words or phrases in Apposition, as,

- Mani, the monitor of VIII class, won the prize.
- Ramoo, the captain of our cricket team, is a fast bowler.

9. To separate the Nominative of Address; as,

- Boys, do not make a noise.
- Don't go there, Susheel.

10. To mark off a direct quotation from the rest of the sentence; as,

- "Look sharp," cried the Superintendent, "Do not waste time."

11. After an Adverb Phrase, a Clause or an Adverb if it precedes the Principal Clause; as,

- As a matter of right, you must fight for it.
- When the old cock rows, the young cock learns.

12. To separate the words yes, no, please, thank you, well; as,

- Yes, I will do it for you.
- No, none has turned up yet.
- Shut the door, please.
- I am quite well, thank you.
- Well, I need your assistance.

13. To separate phrases like weather permitting, God willing, in fact, after all, at last, if they occur in the beginning of the sentence; as,

- Weather permitting, we shall go out for a walk.
- God willing, success shall be ours.
- After all, he is your brother.
- In fact, she accepted my proposal.

14. To separate short Coordinate Clause of a Compound Sentence; as,

- The world is a looking-glass, and it gives back to every man the reflection of his own fact

15. **Use a Comma before any one of the conjunctions (and, but, for, or, neither, nor) when it joins a pair of main clauses.**

- Many are called, but few are chosen.
- He read the book quickly, for he was late.
- She will be there, or I am mistaken.
- He said he would be there, and I do not doubt his word.

16. **Use a comma before and after such elements as for example, to be sure, in fact, however, nevertheless, and therefore when they are used parenthetically.**

- We do not, for example, favour a moratorium.
- He was in fact, unequal to the work.
- She will go, therefore, at six o'clock.

17. **Use a comma to separate thousands, millions, billions, etc. in number of four or more digits.**

3,197	3,284,962
52,012	653,039,253

18. **Use a comma between title and name of organisation where 'of ' or 'of the' has been omitted.**

- Commander, Fourth Army Corps.
- President, University of Delhi.
- Superintendent, Board of Health.

19. **Use a comma before the abbreviations or degrees Jr., Sr., M.A., M.D., Ph.D., etc.**

- John Kennedy, Jr.
- Pramod Julka, M.D.
- Shashikala Chaudhry, Ph.D.

20. **To separate words of the same part of speech in a sentence:**

- Cows, horses, dogs, elephants and camals are all found in India.
- Roses are pink, white, red and yellow.

21. **Before and after words and phrases in apposition:**

- Mrs. Indira Gandhi, the Prime Minister of India, is a lover of peace
- Delhi, the capital of India, is a big city.

22. To separate the words of salutations like Sir, Madam etc.

- May I come in, Sir?

23. To separate phrases and words in a sentence.

- He is, after all, my brother.
- She did not, however, agree with me.
- Man, of course, is a social animal.
- He is, to tell you the truth, a perfect gentleman.

III. THE SEMI-COLON (;)

The Semi-colon shows a pause longer than that of a Comma. It is used;

1. To separate pairs of clauses joined by Commas; as,

- He came home, because he was called; he went away, because he had no work.

2. To mark division of a long Compound Sentence; as,

- Between salary and wages there is much difference; the former is a regular monthly amount; the latter is the remuneration of daily work.

3. To give greater emphasis to the various clauses; as,

- He wants money to spend; friends to talk to; a car to drive about; a bungalow to live in.

4. To separate pairs of words; as,

- bail, bale; tail, tale; hail, hale; mail, male.

5. We use it to separate two clauses of compound sentences, e.g.

- The rick are often miserly; the rich are often cruel.

6. It separate the co-ordinate clauses from the "whereas, for, but, only, therefore, otherwise."

- Work hard; otherwise you will fail.
- She came late; therefore she was fined.
- I went to his house; but he was not there.
- Rani is intelligent; whereas her brother is dull.

IV. THE COLON (:)

The Colon is a mark of punctuation used to introduce a clause or phrase that implifies or is in explanation of a preceding clause. The Colon shows a pause longer than that of Semi-colon but shorter than that of a Full Stop. It is used as;

1. To introduce a quotation or speech; as,

- We all know the proverb: "Might is right."

2. To Separate two opposite clauses; as,

- Man proposes: God disposes.
- To err is human: to forgive divine.

3. Before a list or enumeration of examples; as,

- The following articles were bought: flour, pulses, butter, curd and cheese.

- The following students were absent :
  Poonam, Rajeev, Mohan, Sunny and Veena.

4. Use the colon to express time.

- 8:30 A.M.
- 12:25 P.M.

5. Use the colon in proportions.

- 1:3 3:9
- The ratio was 16:1

6. To separate two contrasted clauses.

- To err is human : to forgive is divine.
- Man proposes : God disposes.

7. **To introduce a number of examples:**

- Their names are : Tom, Dick, and Harry.
- I have to buy the following things :
  A bicycle, a time-piece, a dictionary and a fountain pen.
- Some more important points are : Brevity, Clearity and Correctness.

V. THE SIGN OF INTERROGATION (?)

1. **The Interrogation (?) is used after the direct question; as,**

- What do you want?
- Where do you live?
- Who brought you up?
- How fast are we going?
- "How fast are we going?" He asked.

2. **Use the question mark within the sentence when it is desirable to emphasize each element separately.**

- Where now is his love of country? His political integrity? His unblemished record?

Note- The sign of interrogation is not employed in the following cases.

1. **Not to be used after indirect question.**

- She asked me why I was sitting idle.
- I asked him how old he was.

2. **When the question is really a form of polite request.**

  Will you please pass me the salad.
- Could I have a look your watch, please.

VI. THE SIGN OF EXCLAMATION (!)

1. The sign of Exclamation (!) is used after indirect sentences expressing sudden surprise, joy, sorrow, anger or other feelings; as,

- Alas! I am undone.
- Hurrah! I have won a prize.
- Oh, I were the Prime Minister!
- O God! Have mercy on me.
- Alas! Hurrah! Bravo! Good God!

2. After every optative sentence,

- May you live hundred springs!
- Would that I were a millionaire!

VII. THE INVERTED COMMAS (" ")

1. The inverted commas are used to enclose the actual words of the speaker; as,

- They said, "Be Patriots."
- "What do you want?" She said to the beggar.
- She said to me, "I can not help you in this matter."
- "Talk back your dreadful gift" said Midas, "I do not want gold at all."

2. Name of Books, Poems, Megazines are placed in between inverted Commas.

- I have read Nehru's 'Discovery of India.'
- 'My Native Land' is an inspiring Poem.
- I read the 'Times of India' everyday.

3. Inverted commas are used to emphasize or point out a word in a sentence.

- The word "bear" has several meanings.

VIII. HYPHEN (-)

1. **The Hyphen (-) is used to join th parts of a compound word; as,**

   - Father-in-law, Lookers-on, Passer-by, Commander-in-chief, Neck-lace.

2. **To separate the fractional parts**

   - One-third, Three-fourth, Two-fifth

3. **After Prefix**

   - Sub-Inspector, Vice-Principal, Co-operation.

IX. THE DASH (---)

It should be used only in extreme cases, when other forms of punctuation are inadequate. The dash may often be substituted for the comma, semi-colon, colon mark.

1. **The Dash (---) is used to make a sudden break or change of thought in the sentence; as,**

   - Relatives, friends, companions - all left me my misfortune.

2. **Use a dash when there is repetition for additional or especial emphasis.**

   - We are now faced with a new problem --- the problem of isolating the germ.

3. **The dash is useful at the end of a long series to introduce material concerning that series.**

   - With careful study, with diligent practice, with the desire for improvement --- with all these, one should be able to succeed.

4. **The dash may be used to call attention to a word or group of words following it**

   - He works hard --- too hard, in fact.
   - The American character may be described in one word --- courage.

X. THE APOSTROPHE (')

The apostrophe is used to indicate the omission of one or more letters from a word or to form the possessive of certain nouns as indicated in the following rules.

1. **Use the apostrophe to indicate the omission of one or more letters from a word, or figures from a number.**

   - I can't do it now.
   - He wouldn't do it then.
   - Hon'ble Minister has addressed the nation.

2. **To form the plurals; as,**

   - MA's MLA's
   - Two MLA's live here.
   - Many MA's and BA's are going about in search of employment.

3. **In place of omitted letters.**

   Don't = do not, Won't = will not, Can't = can not
   'Tis = it is, Shan't = shall not, ain't = am not

4. **To show the possessive case of Nouns**

   Mohan's slate; the boy's book

XI. THE BRACKETS ( )

1. **The brackets are used to separate from the main sentence, a phrase or a clause which does not grammatically belong to it as,**

   - At the tender age (such is the power of genius) he could multiply figures of four or five digits.

2. **In reference to tables, diagrams etc.**

   - The cost of living (See Chart II) has risen slowly but surely.

Note: **The part which is used in a bracket intended to be read as a side remark provided the removal of such part would not destroy the sense of the context.**

XII The CAPITAL LETTERS

In Parliamentary debates and other shorthand passages, the following common words / phrases must be capitalised; otherwise one mistake is counted in shorthand tests conducted by various Government Agencies / Institutions:-

- Parliament of India, Council of Ministers, Statement of Objects & Reasons, House for Lok Sabha & Rajya Sabha, Chair of the Speaker or that of the Chairman, Table of the House, Cut Motions, Call Attention Motions, Community Projects, Minutes of Dissent, Lok Sabha, Rajya Sabha, names of all Acts and Bills or the word "Act" or "Bill" represented for any Act or Bill, names of all important Committees, Commissions (Public Accounts Committee, Select Committee, Pay Commissions etc.), Member of Parliament, Mr. Speaker, Mr. Deputy Speaker, Mr. Chairman, Mr. Vice-chairman, Mr. Deputy Chairman, All kinds of salutations e.g. Sir, Madam, Gentlemen, Ladies & Gentlemen, Supreme Court, High Court, Chief Justice Judge of Supreme Court and High Courts, Honourable Member (s), President's Address, President's Rule, Opposition Parties, Constituent Assembly, Article, Rule, Appendix, Annexure, Statement, Directive Principles of State Policy, Fundamental Rights, Scheduled Castes, Scheduled Tribes, First Five Year Plan, Second Five Year Plan and so on, Demands for Grants, Enclosure, Judiciary (but not Judicial), House of Lords, Hon'ble House or hon. House, House of Peoples, Lower House, Leader of the House, Legislature, Legislative Assembly, Motion of Thanks, Member of Legislative Assembly, Ordinance, Presidential Order, Party in Power, Part A, Rule 163, Representation of Peoples, State List, Senator Select Committee, Supplementary Grants, Standing Order, Upper House, Union List, Union Territory, White Paper, Vice-chancellor.

In addition to the above, capital letters must also be used in the following cases also:-

- **Capitalise first letter of every sentence or group of words used as a sentence.**

- **Capitalise every proper noun and also an adjective referring to that proper nouns e.g.**

  Bombay, New Delhi; Pt. Jawahar Lal Nehru, Supreme Court of India, United States of America

- **In a direct form of sentence, the first word in a quotation mark is capitalised e.g.**

  The Chairman said, "The discussions will be resumed after lunch."

- **Capitalise all Gazetted appointments / designations e.g.**

  Under Secretary, Section Officer, Private Secretary, Assistant Director, Joint Secretary.

- **Capitalise personal names and titles - Executive, Professional, Military, Religious and family.**

  Prime Minister, Dr. Manmohan Singh, Shri C. Rajagopalachari, the recipient of Padma Vir Chakra

  General T.N. Raina

  Dr. D.S. Kothari, Chairman Education Commission.

- **Popular Descriptive names that are sometimes used in place of the real proper names should also be capitalised e.g.**

  The Father of the Nation (Mahatma Gandhi)
  The Frontier Gandhi (Khan Abdul Gaffar Khan)
  The Sarvodya Leader (Jaya Prakash Narayan)
  The Windy City (Chicago)

- **Capitalise the names of firms, companies, associations, societies, commissions, committees, bureaus, boards, institutions, departments, schools, political parties, conventions, universities, clubs, fraternities, religious bodies, organisations and unions.**

- **Capitalise days of week, holidays, seasons, months and religious days / festivals.**

- **Capitalise East, West, North and South when they refer to places and do not capitalise when they refer to a directions e.g.**

  Indian Society can not adapt to the fashions of the West.
  The hospital is towards the east direction.

- **Capitalise the names of castes, sub-castes, tribes, religious and language.**

- **Capitalise the names of courses of study. Capitalise academic degrees when used in their abbreviated forms: B.A., M.A. and do not capitalise when used as general designation as a bachelor of arts degree.**

- **Do not capitalise ex - or - elect when used with titles or designation, e.g.**

  ex - Member of Parliament.
  President - elect.

- **Capitalise the names of important historical events, movements, periods, specific treaties, bills, acts and laws e.g.**

  Quit India Movement, Battle of Panipat.

****

Some unpunctuated / punctuated passages are given to familiarise with the rules / procedures of punctuation and capital letters.

1. **Unpunctuated** chennai former tamil nadu chief minister m karunanidhi has refused to apply for bail his lawyer r shanmugasundaram said today karunanidhi said he was ready to face the case in the court shanmugasundaram who called on the dmk leader at the central prison in chennai told mediapersons after a half hour meeting the lawyer said karunanidhi was brought before him in a wheel chair asked about his conversation with the leader shanmugasundaram said I told him that the case was not that of a heinous nature and getting a bail was always possible but he refused asked whether he would insist karunanidhi again to move a bail petition considering his health conditions shanmugasundaram said karunanidhi alone can take a decision in this matter

Punctuated Chennai: Former Tamil Nadu Chief Minister M. Karunanidhi has refused to apply for bail, his lawyer R. Shanmugasundaram said today. "Karunanidhi said he was ready to face the case in the court," Shanmugasundaram, who called on the DMK leader at the Central Prison in Chennai, told mediapersons after a half hour meeting.

The lawyer said Karunanidhi was brought before him in a wheel-chair. Asked about his conversation with the leader, Shanmugasundaram said: "I told him that the case was not that of a heinous nature. And getting a bail was always possible. But he refused."

Asked whether he would insist Karunanidhi again to move a bail petition, considering his health conditions, Shanmugasundaram said: "Karunanidhi alone can take a decision in this matter."

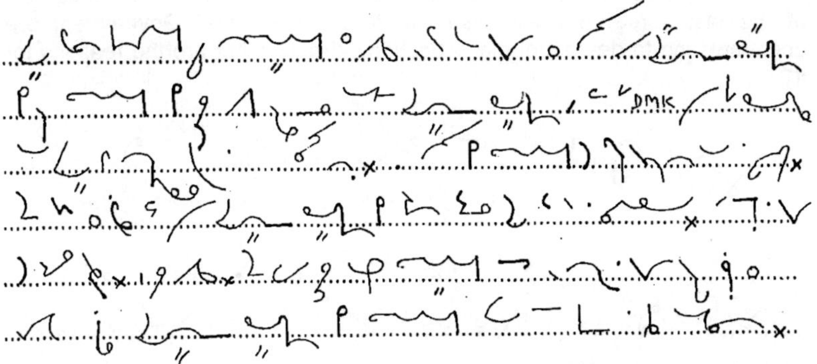

2. **Unpunctuated** mr speaker sir no registration is done with regard to mutual agreement signed between indian universities and foreign universities in the department of human resource development because the universities are run by the state governments however we get the information about the agreements signed by the central universities but only that agreement is legal which is signed in accordance with the act of universities the problem crop up when some foreign universities run thir course through private agents so far we had no power to ban it there was no provision of this kind in university grants commission act that is why we formed a task force to suggest the way to check irregular activities of these universities in the recommendations of the task force proper amendments have been suggested in the university grants commission act over which we are considering and would soon bring a legislation in this regard mr speaker sir i had asked as to what were main recommendations of the task force i would also like to know whetner government are contemplating to decontrol the education if not what are the reasons for it

Punctuated Mr. Speaker, Sir, no registration is done with regard to mutual agreement signed between Indian Universities and foreign Universities in the Department of Human Resource Development because the Universities are run by the State Governments. However, we get the information about the agreements signed by the Central Universities. But only that agreement is legal which is signed in accordance with the Act of Universities. The problem crop up when some foreign Universities run their course through private agents. So far we had no power to ban it. There was no provision of this kind in University Grants Commission Act. That is why we formed a task force to suggest the way to check irregular activities of these Universities. In the recommendations of the task force, proper amendments have been suggested in the University Grants Commission Act, over which we are considering and would soon bring a legislation in this regard.

Mr. Speaker, Sir, I had asked as to what were main recommendations of the task force? I would also like to know whether Government are contemplating to de-control the education. If not, what are the reasons for it?

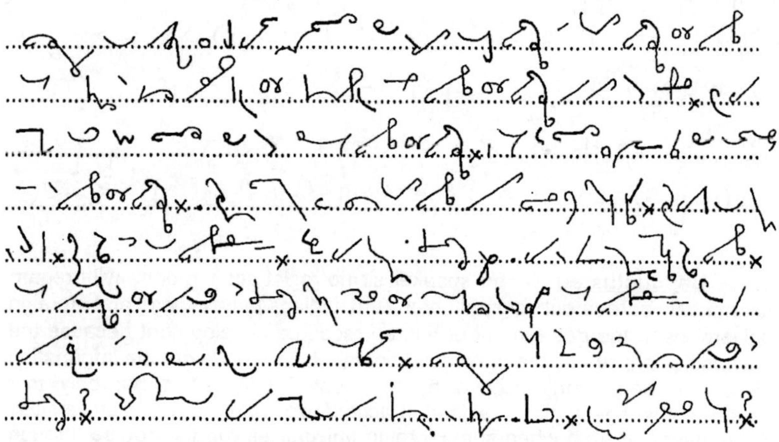

3. Unpunctuated mr deputy speaker sir i am bringing to your kind notice an issue national importance sir the prime minister of india honble shri atal bihari vajpayee has visited pakistan on 20th and 21st february 1999 on inaugural run of the delhi lahore bus service during the visit the prime minister conveyed to the government and the people of pakistan indias deep desire for peace and friendship with them and to develop the comprehensive cooperation for the benefit of the peoples of both the countries the prime minister of india and the prime minister of pakistan signed the lahore declaration which is a designated landmark for peace and security of two countries but later the reactions of the peoples of both the countries which appeared were unpleasant and contrary to the spirit of the lahore declaration this may be because of the ambiguity of the lahore declaration hence it is very much essential to spell out the lahore declaration for the peoples of india and pakistan mr deputy speaker sir i would like to draw the attention of the house towards a very important issue i would like to urge upon the government that this problem should be solved

Punctuated Mr. Deputy Speaker, Sir, I am bringing to your kind notice an issue national importance. Sir, the Prime Minister of India hon'ble Shri Atal Bihari Vajpayee has visited Pakistan on 20th and 21st February, 1999 on inaugural run of the Delhi-Lahore bus service. During the visit, the Prime Minister conveyed to the Government and the people of Pakistan India's deep desire for peace and friendship with them and to develop the comprehensive co-operation for the benefit of the peoples of both the countries. The Prime Minister of India and the Prime Minister of Pakistan signed the Lahore Declaration which is a designated landmark for peace and security of two countries. But later, the reactions of the peoples of both the countries which appeared, were unpleasant and contrary to the spirit of the Lahore Declaration. This may be because of the ambiguity of the Lahore Declaration. Hence, it is very much essential to spell out the Lahore Declaration for the peoples of India and Pakistan.

Mr. Deputy Speaker, Sir, I would like to draw the attention of the House towards a very important issue. I would like to urge upon the Government that this problem should be solved.

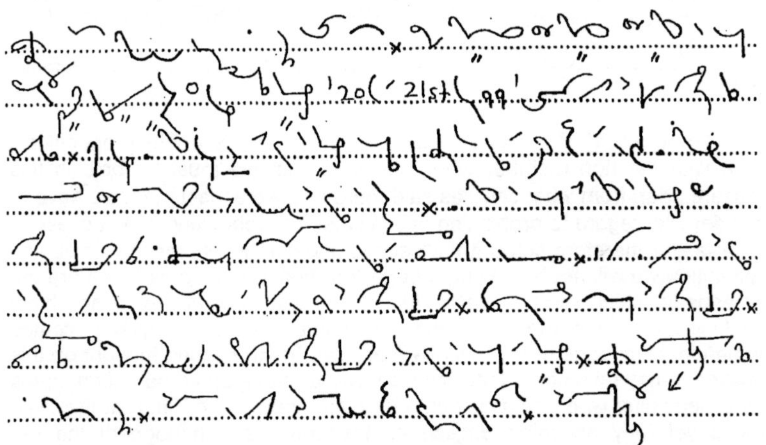

4. **Unpunctuated** the air mail delivery of your magazine alongwith your letter dated 1st january have been received i must congratulate you highly on this production it took a lot of hard work and great ability to produce it and you should and undoubtedly will receive many complements your printers did a splendid job and i find no typographical errors at least in my own little contribution i havent had time as yet to fully ready everything in the magazine i suppose that some time machine shorthand will be introduced in india as it has been in the u s in fact it seem that we shorthand reporters are people who belong to the past in this country however many judges still prefer the pen reporters as do many lawyers

Punctuated The air-mail delivery of your magazine alongwith your letter dated 1st January, have been received. I must congratulate you highly on this production: it took a lot of hard work and great ability to produce it and you should, and undoubtedly will, receive many complements. Your printers did a splendid job and I find no typographical errors, at least in my own little contribution, I haven't had time as yet to fully ready everything in the magazine.

I suppose that some time machine shorthand will be introduced in india, as it has been in the U.S. In fact, it seem that we, shorthand reporters, are people who belong to the past in this country. However, many judges still prefer the pen reporters, as do many lawyers.

5. **Unpunctuated** lastly i will say a few words about prohobition i agree with the hon member when she says that we must be bold in this measure apart from what she has said there are two aspects that we have to consider with regard to prohibition one is whether prohobition is a success or it is a failure therefore scrap it the second question is whether by scrapping prohobition we will not be having a better position in the states these are the two aspects which i would like to deal now though i come froma non hindi speaking area i want to say that we must somehow see that hindi becomes the national language of this country there can be no second thought on this question it may take some time but we have to take it up in the united states in the beginning when colonisation took place there were different linguistic groups yet they accepted english as their national language during the transitional period they had to meet some difficulties but all the same they went through it and solved the question of national language once for all in fact i am ashamed to speak in a language which is not the national language not that i have any hatred for english but it affects self respect

Punctuated Lastly, I will say a few words about prohobition. I agree with the Hon. Member when she says that we must be bold in this measure. Apart from what she has said, there are two aspects that we have to consider with regard to prohibition. One is whether prohobition is a success or " It is failure; therefore, scrap it." The second question is whether by scrapping prohobition we will not be having a better position in the States. These are the two aspects which I would like to deal now.

Though, I come from a non-Hindi speaking area, I want to say that we must somehow see that Hindi becomes the national language of this country. There can be no second thought on this question. It may take some time but we have to take it up. In the United States, in the beginning, when colonisation took place, there were different linguistic groups. Yet, they accepted English as their national language. During the transitional period, they had to meet some difficulties but, all the same, they went through it and solved the question of national language once for all. In fact, I am ashamed to speak in a language which is not the national language; not that I have any hatred for English but it affects self-respect. 185

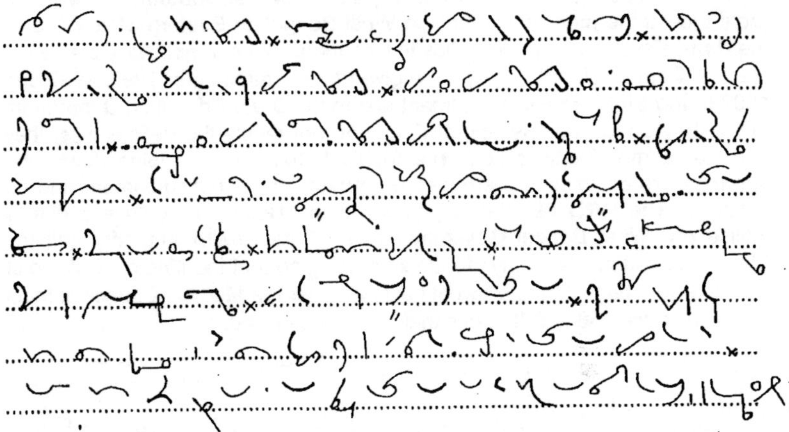

6. **Unpunctuated** mr deputy speaker sir i was trying to draw your attention to a very disturbing news item appeared in todays the hindustan times about the calcutta medical college as we all know the calcutta medical college is the oldest medical college in this country and has been the premier institution in asia the hindustan times of today says that the medical council of india has drastically reduced the number of seats in the mbbs course from 155 to 100 I have been an educationist all my life I can tell you that this will be a great blow tothe medical students in west bengal in easter states and all the north eastern states why has this happened I can not really blame the medical council of india they have given three warnings in 1993 1997 and 1998 to the state health department and to the state education department that if they do not do anything or if they do not rectify the deficiencies they will take some drastic action the medical college was going down the buildings are collapsing there are no infrastructure no equipment and no

teaching the hrd minister is present in the house I would ask him to advise our west bengal government the state health authority and the state education authority to do something so that the medical college of calcutta gets back its pride I would also request the medical council of india to give us back 150 mbbs seats that we originally had

Punctuated Mr. Deputy Speaker, Sir, I was trying to draw your attention to a very disturbing news item appeared in today's The Hindustan Times about the Calcutta Medical College.

As we all know, the Calcutta Medical College is the oldest medical college in this country and has been the premier institution in Asia. The Hindustan Times of today says that the Medical Council of India has drastically reduced the number of seats in the MBBS course from 155 to 100. I have been an educationist all my life. I can tell you that this will be a great blow tothe medical students in West Bengal, in Eastern States and all the North-Eastern States. Why has this happened? I can not really blame the Medical Council of India. They have given three warnings in 1993, 1997 and 1998 to the State Health Department and to the State Education Department that if they do not do anything or if they do not rectify the deficiencies, they will take some drastic action. The Medical College was going down; the buildings are collapsing; there was no infrastructure, no equipment and no teaching. The HRD Minister is present in the House. I would ask him to advise our West Bengal Government, the State Health Authority and the State Education Authority to do something so that the Medical College of Calcutta gets back its pride I would also request the Medical Council of India to give us back 150 MBBS seats that we originally had.

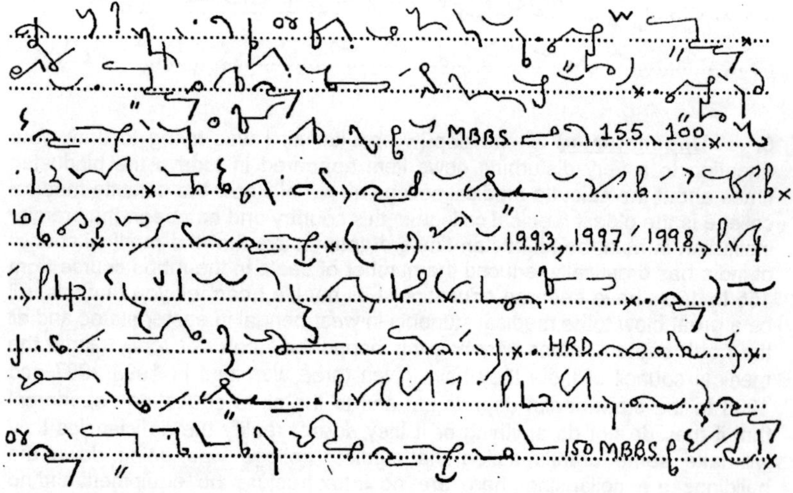

7. **Unpunctuated** mr deputy speaker sir i would like to draw the attention of this august house to a very serious matter the food corporation of india is transporting substandard and damaged foodgrains to kerala which are not actually having the required quality it is substandard and it is not fit for human consumption sir it is a matter of common knowledge that foodgrains had been damaged in large quantity in andhra pradesh and being procured by the food corporation of india and deported to kerala and from last january onwards the damaged rice which is not fit for human consumption is allotted to kerala for the public distribution system this is done at a time when the government of india has increased the issue price of foodgrains meant for distribution through the public distribution system mr deputy speaker sir through you i want to draw the attention of the government towards the fact that even 10 per cent of the funds given under various schemes in which the grants of the members of parliament and member of legislative assemblies could also be included is not spent on development work

Punctuated Mr. Deputy Speaker, Sir, I would like to draw the attention of this August House to a very serious matter. The Food Corporation of India is transporting substandard and damaged foodgrains to Kerala which are not actually having the required quality. It is substandard and it is not fit for human consumption.

Sir, it is a matter of common knowledge that foodgrains had been damaged in large quantity in Andhra Pradesh and being procured by the Food Corporation of India and deported to Kerala and from last January onwards, the damaged rice, which is not fit for human consumption, is allotted to Kerala for the Public Distribution System. This is done at a time when the Government of India has increased the issue price of foodgrains meant for distribution through the Public Distribution System.

Mr. Deputy Speaker, Sir, through you, I want to draw the attention of the Government towards the fact that even 10 per cent of the funds given under various schemes, in which the grants of the Members of Parliament and Member of Legislative Assemblies could also be included is not spent on development work.

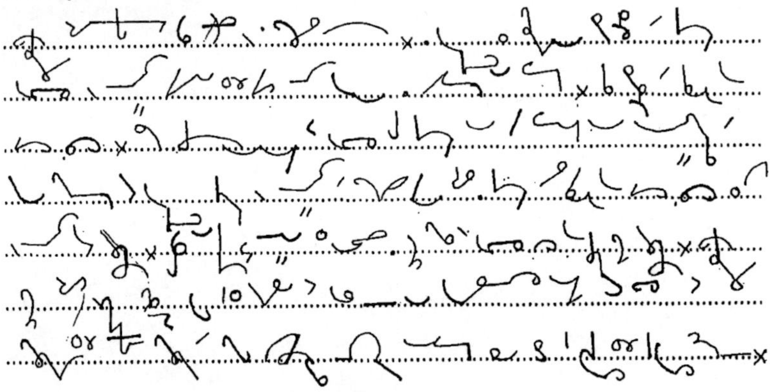

Marking of Mistakes

How to mark & analyse the mistakes in Shorthand passages, Analysis Sheet of Mistakes for day-to-day improvement.

MARKING OF MISTAKES

To achieve the highest speed with accuracy, the following points must be kept in mind by the learners/high speed aspirants having the knowledge of marking of mistakes.

1. Every word omitted or added is an **Error.**

2. Substitution of one or more words in place of one right word is to be taken as one **Error**, e.g. **As Well As** written in place of **Swallows** is counted as one **Error**. In the converse case, this is taken as three **Errors**, e.g. **Swallows** written in place of **As Well As** is counted as three mistakes.

3. Every word mis-spelt is an **Error**, but if the same word is mis-spelt and repeated several times, an additional error need not be counted. Only one mistake is counted.

   Proper noun mis-spelt need not be marked as **Errors**, unless they represent well-known names like Nehru, Gandhi.

4. An **Error** should be marked where a word is broken into parts, like **can not** instead of **cannot or can't**, or where words are wrongly compounded, as **inspite of** instead of **in spite of**.

5. Omission of Full Stop / Period at the end of a sentence or wrong position of Full Stop / period is as an **Error** and two mistakes are counted.

6. Omission of period after abbreviations like viz., etc., is also an **Error.**

7. Omission of Interrogation or Exclamation mark is an **Error.**

8. Omission of other punctuation marks like comma, semi-colon, colon, hyphen and dash need not be counted as **Error.** But if these punctuation marks are omitted or inserted in such a manner that the sense of the sentence is changed thereby, then Error should be marked for every such wrong punctuation. In some cases, essential commas and hyphens are required to be placed, otherwise, it is counted as an Error.

9. Omission or wrong position of the "apostrophe" should be marked as an **Error.**

10. Proper noun should begin with capital letters, otherwise they are marked as an **Error.**

    All the shorthand trainees/students should read the Chapter **"Punctuation and Capital Letters"** carefully & attentively and always use the capital letters for the words / phrases given in this Chapter, otherwise, it is also counted as **an Error.**

11. Paragraphs in a transcription need not be exactly like the original passage but it should be in a systematic manner. If the candidate has not made paragraphs at all, two additional **Errors** are counted.

12. Typographical Errors like the words being mis-spelt or repeated, or omission of space between words, over-typing, crowding, faulty shifting and trans-position of words or letters and other typing mistakes are counted as **Errors.**

13. During transcribe the shorthand passage, care must be taken to type a word in its full form or in an abbreviated form, as it is dictated. For example, the word **'UP'** instead of **'Uttar Pradesh'**, or **'UK'** instead of **'United Kingdom'** or **'don't** instead of **'do not'** are counted as mistake.

14. Shabby erasing during transcribe the passage should be penalised as an **Error**. But in the Typing Test it is not allowed.

15. Every cancellation with overtyping or **'X'** ing will be counted as an **Error.**

16. Neat insertions or additions between lines or in the margin by typing are not counted as **Errors.** The insertions / additions should be marked as **Errors,** if they are done with pen or pencil.

17. If the candidate has a sprawling and untidy style or writing his shorthand notes and is extravagant in the use of note book, two additional **Errors** should be counted.

Criteria of marking the mistakes

The approved criteria for selection of candidates @ 80/100/120 w.p.m. in Shorthand Test is that the candidates are required to commit the mistake (s) less than 5% of the passage dictated.

But if the learners/high speed aspirants wants to acquire the shorthand speed perfectly in a short time, the standard of efficiency may put them in the following categories:

Percentage of Errors	Category
Without mistake	**Outstanding**
Less than 1%	Excellent
Between 1% to 2%	Very Good
Between 2% to 3%	Good
Between 3% to 4%	Satisfactory
Between 4% to 5%	Average
More than 5%	Failed

To achieve the desired target, the learners/high speed aspirants may also maintain the date-wise **"Mistakes Analysis Sheet"** containing the column of punctuations and other common mistakes which are frequently committed by them daily in the shorthand dictated passage.

A proforma of **"Mistakes Analysis Sheet"** is also given so that the learners/high speed aspirants may easily analyse their daily mistakes and practise the same to achieve the accuracy in dictation. The break-up of mistakes is given below:

i. Full Stop, **ii.** Interrogation, **iii.** Exclamation, **iv.** Semi-colon, **v.** Hyphen, **vi.** Dash, **vii.** Colon, **viii.** Apostrophe, **ix.** Inverted Commas, **x.** Brackets, **xi.** Para, **xii.** Comma, **xiii.** Capital/Small letters, **xiv.** Spelling, **xv.** Singular/Plural, **xvi.** Shortforms/Grammalogues, **xvii.** Contractions/Phraseography, **xviii.** Typographical, **xix.** Mis-hearing/Mis-reading, **xx.** Missing,

****

TRANSCRIPTION MISTAKES ANALYSIS SHEET

NAME____________________ MONTH____________

Date	Speed	MISTAKES																									Remarks	Chart of Repeating Mistakes
		Punctuations												Other Common Mistakes														
		Full Stop (.)	Interrogation (?)	Exclamation (!)	Semi-colon (;)	Hyphen (-)	Dash (-)	Colon (:)	Apostrophe (')	Inverted Commas (" ")	Brackets ( )	Para (//)	Comma (,)	Capital/Small	Spelling	Singular/Plural	Shortforms /Grammalogues	Contractions/ Phraseography	Typographical	Mis-hearing/mis-reading	Missing	Total Words	Total Mistakes	Time Permissible	Time Taken	% age of mistakes		
1	2	3	4	5	6	7	8	9	10	11	12	13	14	15	16	17	18	19	20	21	22	23	24	25	26	27	28	29

Special outlines

Definition of phraseography, its proper use, advanced outlines of important & common phrases related to different fields.

Phraseography

The joining of two or more than two words written without lifting the pencil or pen is called **"Phrase"**. The outline, thus, is called *phraseogram. The position of a phrase is determined from the position of the first word.*

In stenography, each outline was written separately when the Pitman Shorthand was first invented and implemented in 1837 but after some time outlines are joined together to make a phrase by omitting some of the words. It is well known that today we can not imagine shorthand writing without phraseography and all shorthand learners/high speed aspirants use phrasing to a greater extent compatile with facile writing and assured legitibility.

The advantage of phrasing are at once apparent when we compare the following ways of writing in the sentence: **I shall be glad if you will consider the matter.**

In the sentence, if each outline is written separately, the shorthand rendering is:

(i) **I** .... **shall** .... **be** ...... **glad** ...... **if** .... **you** .... **will** .... **consider** .... **the** .... **matter** ....

In this example, we have ten separate outlines of nine lifts of the pen/pencil having several changes of position in relation to the line of writing.

(ii) If phrasing is used, the shorthand may become:

I Shall be glad .... **if you will** .... **consider the matter** ....

In this example, we have only three outlines with two lifts of the pen/pencil with good lineality.

(iii) If the writer is more advanced, the shorthand may become:

I Shall be glad if you will consider the matter ....

In this example, we have only one outline without lifting pen/pencil which is to be used when we are taking the dictation @ speed of 120 w.p.m. and above.

We have seen that the saving of time in the second and third examples is immense not only because the phrases are written quickly but also becuase the hand has travelled so short of a distance as is the time taken to write outline to outline separately.

The following classes of phrases should be used to the fullest extent after completing the textbook.

1. Those phrases in which outlines are simply joined together without any change of form.

I am glad .... **I shall have** .... **do you** ....

may we .... **with which** .... **that is not** ....

we will .... **last year** ....

2. Those phrases in which one or more of the outlines making up the phrase are written differently by adopting the omission of words.

able to .... **better than** .... **at all** .... **in our** .... **of the world** .... **of us** .... **as we may** ....

if it were ....

3. Those phrases in which one or more of the outlines comprising the phrase is ommitted but there is no change in the remaining outlines.

for a time .... **more or less** .... **larger and larger** ....

Phraseograms may be formed by **(i) simple joining, (ii) by changing the form of one or more of the outlines or (iii) by omission** of one part or the whole by adopting the following points which may usefully be elaborated.

1. The phrases must have good linearity. It should not ascend too far above nor descend too far below the line of writing.

2. The phrases should be simple and easy to write. Always avoid awkward joinings which can not be written easily.

3. Each outline should be clearly distinguishable and the part should not blend into one which is unrecognisable sign.

4. Words which are flow together in speech may be represented as a phrase in shorthand but words which are clearly separated by giving a pause in speech should not be represented by phrase/ joined outlines in shorthand.

5. The first outline of a phraseograms retains its correct position in relation to the line of writing, but the position of the following strokes/outlines is governed by the preceding outline or outlines. Phrase should not drop more than two strokes below and above the line.

6. Phrases should not be complicated and should not be used for long sentences. Such phrasing joining are not clear & distinguishable and always lead to confusion in transcription.

<u>How to distinguish the phrases</u>

In some cases the consonantal structure of two forms is similar and position writing affords no guidance to make the phrases perfectly. For this, learners/slow speed aspirants may use the vowel indication or disjoining the consonant to make some distinction in those outlines/phrases which are similar in writing.

So to make the phrases perfectly, the procedure, as is given, may be adopted

By vowel indication

At last	....	At least	....
By any means	....	By no means	....
For me	....	For him	....
From me	....	From him	....
To me	....	To him	....
You will say	....	You will see	....
Let us say	....	Let us see	....
In another case	....	In neither case	....
In any case	....	In no case	....
We had not	....	We do not	....
We did not	....	We do'nt	....
To give	....	To go	....
We give	....	We go	....
Young man	....	Young men	....
It is most probable	....	It seems probable	....
For those	....	For this/For these	....
To those	....	To this/to these	....
When those	....	When this	....
When these	....		

By disjoining

I know	....	I note	....
We know	....	We note	....
Know this	....	Note this	....
I may	....	I might	....
It may	....	It might	....
In all cases	....	In two cases	....
It can be	....	It could be	....
I can be	....	I could be	....
Who can be	....	Who could be	....
For the year	....	In the year	....
Very well	....	Very ill	....
It is unnecessary	....	It is not necessary	....
It is unnatural	....	It is not natural	....
It is known	....	It is not known	....
It is in-convenient	....	It is not convenient	....
It is unfinished	....	It is not finished	....
We are unable to	....	We are not able to	....

Other examples of similar phrases

I regard	....	I regret	....
We regard	....	We regret	....

In my own way	....	In many ways	....
In the course of time	....	In course of time	....
If there is	....	For there is	....
If it	....	For it	....
In other ways	....	Any other ways	....
Large part of	....	Large number of	....
Very much	....	Very large	....
So much	....	So large	....
Too much	....	Too large	....
In a position	....	In the position	....
Unable to	....	Enabled to	....

- **Past tenses**

The past tense of a contracted form may be indicated where considered necessary by writing a small disjoined tick of the contraction.

I expect	....	I expected	....
I respect	....	I respected	....
I represent	....	I represented	....
We inform	....	We informed	....

II Phrases should also be used to represent very common words as given in the chapter of Introduction. Some of the examples are:-

i. **The** - represented by a small tick written either upwards or downwards at a sharp angle:

In the .... with the .... for the .... and the ....

on the .... pay the .... take the ....

ii. **I** - represented by writing the first part of the sign only means initial tick represented for 'I' :

I can .... I am .... I believe .... I want ....

I went .... I agree ....

iii. **He** - represented medially or finally by a short downstroke :

that he may .... for he .... If he .... When he ....

iv. **Much** - represented by stroke **m** and **ch** :

How much .... too much .... so much ....

very much ....

v. **Will** - represented by upward **'L'** :

I will .... You will .... They will .... It will ....

He will .... They will be ....

vi. **Us** - represented by circle **'s"** :

To us ...... for us .... To give us .... Charge us ....

vii. **S-w, S-s** - represented by large circle :

As well as .... As we have .... This is .... As i .... Is as ...... As soon as ....

viii. **Were** - represented by strokes **w** & **ray** :

we were .... they were .... you were ....

ix. **Are** - represented by initial hook **'R'** :

they are ....

x. **Been, than, own** -represented by final hook **'N'** :

have been .... had been .... better than ....

more than .... rather than .... our own ....

their own ....

xi. **Have, of** - represented by final hook **f/v** :

Which have .... Who have .... Out of ....

Number of .... Rate of ....

xii. **Not, To** - represented by halving and by hook **'n'** :

I am not .... I will not .... I can not .... I do not .... I did not .... Had not .... We will not ....

we can not .... we do not .... we did not .... you will not .... you can not .... were not .... may not be .... able to ....

xiii. **Must** - represented by stroke **'m'** and circle **'s'** :

Must be .... Must not be ....

xiv. **Con** - represented by writing the outline close to the preceding stroke/outlines :

In connection .... In control .... In consideration .... We consider .... we continue .... this company .... this committee .... I will comfort ....

it is common .... in condition ....

xv. **Their, there, other** - represented by doubling the stroke preceding these words :

In their .... I am sure there is .... Some other

.... I think there is ....

xvi. **Hundred, thousand, millions and billions** are represented by strokes **n, th, m** and **b** respectively :

700	=	...7.....	7000	=	..7........
7 Million	=	...7.....	7 Billion	=	..7......

Most of the above phrases covers in the shorthand text-book as is explained in the chapter - **'Introduction'.** The following lists of phrases show standard phrases for various fields of interest. Shorthand writers may practise & memorise all these phrases, as also to select and practise those that are likely to be useful in their particular spheres of activity.

Shorthand learners / high speed aspirants may have to select those phrases which are written conveniently as is given in this chapter. So my advice to all the learners / high speed aspirants that they must have to keep at first to the principles of phrasing to acquire the shorthand speed perfectly in a short time.

1. ACCORDING TO

According to the ....

According to this ....

According to these ....

According to me ....

According to him ....

According to them ....

According to that ....

2. ACCOUNT

In the current account ....

Take into account ....

Taken into account ....

Takes into account ....

Taking into account ....

Will be taken into account ....

Would be taken into account ....

3. ADDITION / ADDITIONAL

Additions and alterations ....

Additional expenditure ....

Additional taxes ....

Additional revenue ....

Additional capacity ....

In addition to the ....

In addition to this ....

In addition to that ....

In addition to these ....

In addition to their ....

In addition to all this ....

4. ALSO

Are also ....

Also been ....

Has also been ....

Had also been ....

Have also been ....

Has also to be ....

I have also tried ....

It will also ....

It is also ....

It has also been ....

It has also to be ....

It must also be ....

May also be ....

Must also ....

Must also be ....

Should also ....

There is also ....

They must also ....

Were also ....

We have also ....

We have also to consider ....

We have also to consider the matter ....

We have also tried ....

We have also requested ....

Will also be ....

5. ALL

All of us ....

At all efforts ....

At all our own ....

At all events ....

At first cost ....

At all costs ....

At all levels ....

By all means ....

6. AND SO

And so on ....

And so forth ....

And so on & so forth ....

7. APPEAR

It appears ....

It appears to me ....

It appears that ....

It appears to have been ....

It may appear that ....

8. APART

Apart from the ....

Apart from this ....

Apart from these ....

Apart from that ....

Apart from the fact that ....

Apart from other ....

Apart from other things ....

9. ARRANGE/MENT/S

Adequate arrangement/s ....

Effective arrangement/s ....

Formal arrangement/s ....

Financial arrangement/s ....

Law & Order arrangement/s ....

Local arrangement/s ....

Personal arrangement/s ....

Please make arrangement/s ....

Permanent arrangement/s ....

Temporary arrangement/s ....

There is/are no arrangement/s ....

Who will arrange ....

Who will arrange the matter ....

Which was arranged ....

Which were arranged ....

10. ASSOCIATION

Article of Association ....

Backward Classes' Association ....

Bank Employees' Association ....

Clerk's Association ....

Incorporated Association ....

Land Owners' Association ....

Literary Association ....

Manufacturers' Association ....

Medical Association ....

Memorandum of Association ....

Mine Owners' Association ....

Mill Owners' Association ....

Officers Association . . . .

Political Association . . . .

Scientific Association . . . .

Social Workers' Association . . . .

Teachers Association . . . .

Trade Association . . . .

Trade Merchants Association . . . .

Traders Association . . . .

Welfare Association . . . .

Workers' Association . . . .

11. <u>AS YOU</u>

As you know . . . .

As you know Sir . . . .

As you know very well . . . .

As you all know . . . .

As you know we are . . . .

As you know we have . . . .

As you are . . . .

As you are aware . . . .

As you are not . . . .

As you were . . . .

As you were not . . . .

12. AS I

As I said

As I said Sir

As I have

As I have said

As I have to state

As I have received

As I have not

As I have not been

As I understand

As I have already said

As I have already referred

As I have already told you

13. AS WE

As we are

As we are aware

As we have been

As we have seen

As we have stated

As we have said

As we shall

As we shall not

As we can

As we can not ....

As we do ....

As we do not ....

As we do not know ....

As we do not want ....

As we had ....

As we may also ....

As we wish ....

As we trust ....

As we find ....

As we think ....

As we go ....

As we go into ....

As we go into the matter ....

14. BEGINNING

At the beginning / of the ....

At the very beginning ....

At the beginning of the year ....

At the beginning of the war ....

From the beginning ....

From the very beginning ....

From the beginning to the end ....

In the beginning ....

In the very beginning ....

Right from the beginning ....

Right from the very beginning ....

Since the beginning of ....

Since the beginning of the ....

To begin with ....

Till the beginning of ....

15. BEHALF

In our behalf ....

In this behalf ....

On behalf of the ....

On behalf of the Govt. ....

On behalf of the Govt. of India ....

On their behalf ....

On behalf of their ....

16. BEST

Best of your ability ....

Best of our ability ....

Best of my ability ....

Best of their ability ....

Best of your knowledge ....

Best of my knowledge ....

Best of your capacity ....

Best of my capacity ....

Best of our capacity ....

Best way of ....

Best advantage ....

Best wishes ....

With best wishes ....

17. BUDGET

Budget documents ....

Budget Session ....

Budget discussion ....

Budget speech ....

Budget estimates ....

Budget proposal ....

Common's Budget ....

Defence Budget ....

Farmer's Budget ....

Post Budget ....

Railway Budget ....

General Budget ....

18. CAPACITY

Best of our capacity ....

Best of my capacity ....

Best of your capacity ....

Below the capacity

Existing Capacity

Earning capacity

Generating Capacity

Generation capacity

In our capacity

In my capacity

In your capacity

In their capacity

In his capacity

In its capacity

Idle capacity

Installed capacity

In official capacity

More capacity

Overall capacity

Remarkable capacity

Storage capacity

Utilised capacity

Unutilised capacity

19. CASES

In any case

In no case

In all cases

In all such cases . . . .

In all these cases . . . .

In this case . . . .

In these cases . . . .

In those cases . . . .

In each case . . . .

In which case . . . .

In some cases . . . .

In many cases . . . .

In the case of / the . . . .

In certain cases . . . .

In certain other cases . . . .

If that is the case . . . .

If we take the case / of . . . .

Number of cases . . . .

Take the case of / the . . . .

There are number of cases . . . .

That is the case . . . .

This is the case . . . .

This is not the case . . . .

20. CIRCUMSTANCES

Adverse circumstances . . . .

Auspicious circumstances . . . .

All the circumstances . . . .

Every circumstances ....

Favourable circumstances ....

In the circumstances ....

In the present circumstances ....

In these circumstances ....

In all circumstances ....

In any circumstances ....

In those circumstances ....

In these circumstances ....

Peculiar circumstances ....

Present circumstances ....

Special circumstances ....

Suspicious circumstances ....

Such circumstances ....

Unforeseen circumstances ....

Under the circumstances ....

Under all circumstances ....

Under these circumstances ....

Under those circumstances ....

Under the present circumstances ....

21. CLASS / ES

All class ....

All classes ....

Backward classes ....

Coaching classes . . . .

First class . . . .

First class passengers . . . .

In certain classes . . . .

Lower class . . . .

Lower Middle class . . . .

Middle class . . . .

Middle class people . . . .

Second class . . . .

Second class passengers . . . .

Second class ticket . . . .

Second class fare . . . .

Superior class . . . .

Second class compartment . . . .

Upper class . . . .

Upper class people . . . .

Upper Middle class . . . .

22. <u>COMMISSION</u>

Agricultural Prices Commission . . . .

Administrative Reforms Commission . . . .

Atomic Energy Commission . . . .

Backward Classes Commission . . . .

Banking Commission . . . .

Boundary Commission ....

Central Pay Commission ....

Central Water & Power Commission ....

Commission of Enquiry ....

Election Commission ....

Election Commission of India ....

Enquiry Commission ....

Finance Commission ....

Fiscal Commission ....

High Commission ....

Indian High Commission ....

Khadi Commission ....

Law Commission ....

Oil & Natural Commission ....

Oil & Natural Gas Commission ....

Pakistan High Commission ....

Planning Commission ....

Public Service Commission ....

Railway Service Commission ....

States Reorganisation Commission ....

State Public Service Commission ....

Taxation Enquiry Commission ....

Tariff Commission ....

U. P. S. C. ....

Union Public Service Commission ....

U. G. C. . . . .

University Grants Commission . . . .

Vigilance Commission . . . .

Central Vigilance Commission . . . .

23. CORPORATION

Delhi Corporation . . . .

Food Corporation of India . . . .

Industrial Development Corporation . . . .

Industrial Finance Corporation . . . .

Jute Corporation of India . . . .

Life Insurance Corporation . . . .

Life Insurance Corporation of India . . . .

Metropolitan Corporation . . . .

Municipal Corporation of Delhi . . . .

Municipal Corporation of India . . . .

Municipal Corporation . . . .

National Seeds Corporation . . . .

Statutory Corporation . . . .

State Industrial Corporation . . . .

State Trading Corporation . . . .

24. COMMITTEE

Goods Traffic Committee . . . .

High Level Committee . . . .

High Power Committee

Joint Select Committee

Locomotive & Engineering Committee

Municipal Committee

Pradesh Congress Committee

Public Committee

Public Accounts Committee

Passenger Traffic Committee

Select Committee

Working Committee

25. CONSIDERATION

Active consideration

Above all consideration

After careful consideration

Basic consideration

Careful consideration

Carefully consideration

Can be taken into consideration

Economic consideration

For consideration

For your consideration

For sympathetic consideration

Further consideration

Human consideration

Has to be taken into consideration . . . .
Have to be taken into consideration . . . .
Into consideration . . . .
Little consideration . . . .
Moral consideration . . . .
Of your consideration . . . .
Some consideration . . . .
Special consideration . . . .
Sympathetic consideration . . . .
Shall be taken into consideration . . . .
Should be taken into consideration . . . .
Take into consideration . . . .
Taken into consideration . . . .
Taking into consideration . . . .
Took into consideration . . . .
To be taken into consideration . . . .
Under the consideration . . . .
Under active consideration . . . .
Utmost consideration . . . .
Very careful consideration . . . .
Very serious consideration . . . .
Will be taken into consideration . . . .
Which will be taken into consideration . . . .
Which may be taken into consideration . . . .
Which must be taken into consideration . . . .

26. COME/CAME/COMING

Come into'being ....

Came into being ....

Come into power ....

Came into power ....

Come to an end ....

Came to an end ....

Come up for discussion ....

Came up for discussion ....

Come to light ....

Came to light ....

Come to force ....

Come into force ....

Came into force ....

Coming into force ....

Come into operation ....

Comes into operation ....

Come into existence ....

Came into existence ....

Come forward ....

Comes forward ....

Came forward ....

Come to the conclusion ....

Came to the conclusion ....

Come to the same conclusion ....

Come to a satisfactory conclusion . . . .

In the coming year . . . .

In the coming days . . . .

In the coming months . . . .

In the coming generation . . . .

27. CONSIDER/CONSIDERED

Being considered . . . .

Can be considered . . . .

Can not be considered . . . .

Carefully considered . . . .

Duly considered . . . .

Further considered . . . .

Has to be considered . . . .

Have to be considered . . . .

It is considered . . . .

It is to be considered . . . .

If we consider the . . . .

If we consider the matter . . . .

I do consider . . . .

I do consider that . . . .

I will consider the matter . . . .

I would consider . . . .

I would consider the matter . . . .

Let us consider . . . .

Let us consider the matter . . . .

May be considered . . . .

May not be considered . . . .

Must be considered . . . .

Ought to be considered . . . .

Shall be considered . . . .

Should be considered . . . .

Will be considered . . . .

Which may be considered . . . .

Which are considered . . . .

Which were considered . . . .

Which will be considered . . . .

Which may be considered . . . .

Were considered . . . .

We are considering . . . .

We may consider . . . .

You may consider . . . .

You may consider the matter . . . .

28. COURSE

In course of time . . . .

In due course . . . .

In due course of time . . . .

In the course of the . . . .

In the course of speech . . . .

In the course of his speech . . . .

In the course of his reply . . . .

In the course of discussion . . . .

29. CONCLUSION/CONCLUDED

Come to the conclusion . . . .

Comes to the conclusion . . . .

Came to the conclusion . . . .

Come to the same conclusion . . . .

Come to a satisfactory conclusion . . . .

Certain conclusion . . . .

He has concluded . . . .

I have concluded . . . .

In conclusion . . . .

Logical conclusion . . . .

Necessary conclusion . . . .

Satisfactory conclusion . . . .

That conclusion . . . .

Unsatisfactory conclusion . . . .

We have concluded . . . .

30. CONCERNED

Are concerned . . . .

All concerned . . . .

All those who are concerned ....

All those who were concerned ....

By all concerned ....

Deeply concerned ....

Great concern ....

Greatly concerned ....

Is concerned ....

I am concerned ....

I am greatly concerned ....

It is concerned ....

It may concern ....

It is their concern ....

Primary concern ....

So far as Government is concerned ....

Vitally concerned ....

Very much concerned ....

We are concerned ....

Who are concerned ....

Was concerned ....

Were concerned ....

31. CONNECTION

In connection with ....

In connection with the ....

In connection with their ....

32. DIFFERENT / DIFFERENCE

Different parts of India ....

Different parts of Country ....

Different parts of the City ....

Different parts of the State ....

Different parts of the World ....

Difference of opinion ....

Differences of opinion ....

33. DIRECTION

In my direction ....

In the direction of ....

In that direction ....

In this direction ....

In what direction ....

In many directions ....

In all directions ....

In various directions ....

In these directions ....

In the right direction ....

In any other direction ....

In a different direction ....

In a particular direction ....

In a certain direction ....

In the opposite direction . . . .

In the other direction . . . .

In the same direction . . . .

In the wrong direction . . . .

Misdirection . . . .

Towards that direction . . . .

Under the direction of . . . .

34. DISPOSAL

At the disposal . . . .

At my disposal . . . .

At your disposal . . . .

At their disposal . . . .

At our disposal . . . .

Final disposal . . . .

Immediate disposal . . . .

Supply & disposal . . . .

35. DOUBLE WORDS

Again & Again . . . .

By & By . . . .

By the By . . . .

By and Large . . . .

Crores & Crores . . . .

Deeper & Deeper . . . .

Door to Door . . . .

Every now & then . . . .

East & West . . . .

Economic & Social . . . .

Each & Every . . . .

Face to Face . . . .

Faster & Faster . . . .

Further & Further . . . .

Greater & Greater . . . .

Here & There . . . .

Higher & Higher . . . .

Less & Less . . . .

Larger & Larger . . . .

Lower & Lower . . . .

Millions & Millions . . . .

More & More . . . .

North & South . . . .

Nearer & Nearer . . . .

One by One . . . .

Over & Above . . . .

Over & Over again . . . .

Over & Over Again . . . .

Place to Place . . . .

Part & Parcel . . . .

Plan to Plan . . . .

Rates & Taxes ....

Right or Wrong ....

Step by Step ....

Six or Seven ....

Such & Such ....

Side by Side ....

Time & Space ....

Village to Village ....

Ways & Means ....

Weeks & Weeks ....

Year after Year ....

Year to Year ....

36. DURING THE

During the last ....

During the year ....

During the last year ....

During the last few years ....

During the last two years ....

During the last two or three years ....

During the last few months ....

During the last few days ....

During the last five years ....

During the last five year plan ....

During the past year ....

During the current year

During the year under review

During the coming years

During the coming months

During the coming weeks

During the next month

During the next few months

During the next week

During the next few weeks

During the next few days

During the next few years

During the course of

During the course of discussion

During the course of the debate

During the course of speech

During the course of the year

During the period of war

During the course of the war

During the days of

During the days of the

During the last session

37. EDUCATION

Adult Education

Basic Education

Child Education ....

College Education ....

Compulsory Education ....

Central Board of Education ....

Central Board of School Education ....

Central Board of Secondary Education ....

Department of Education ....

Education Department ....

Elementary Education ....

Higher Education ....

Higher Secondary Education ....

Medium of Education ....

Non-technical Education ....

Political Education ....

Primary Education ....

Present System of Education ....

School Education ....

Standard of Education ....

Scientific Education ....

Secondary Education ....

Senior Secondary Education ....

Technical Education ....

Technical & Scientific Education ....

Universal Education ....

University Education ....

University & College Education ....

38. EFFECT

Came into effect ....

Into effect ....

Psychological effect ....

Retrospective effect ....

Side effect ....

Take effect ....

Take effect from the ....

Took effect from ....

To this effect ....

To that effect ....

With effect from / the ....

With immediate effect ....

With retrospective effect ....

39. ESSENTIAL

Absolutely essential ....

Essential services ....

Essential articles ....

Essential steps ....

Essential supplies ....

Essential Commodities ....

Essential Commodities Act ....

It is essential

It is also essential

It is absolutely essential

Most essential

Very essential

40. EXTENT

Fullest possible extent

Lowest possible extent

Minimum extent

To an extent

To the extent

To that extent

To some extent

To a certain extent

To a great extent

To the extent possible

To this extent

To a greater extent

To such an extent

To a considerable extent

To a large extent

To a larger extent

To a limited extent

To a small extent . . . .

To a vast extent . . . .

Upto the extent . . . .

Upto a certain extent . . . .

41. EXCHANGE

Exchange Policy . . . .

Exchange regulation . . . .

Exchange rate . . . .

Foreign Exchange . . . .

Foreign Exchange Position . . . .

Foreign Exchange requirements . . . .

Foreign Exchange Resources . . . .

Foreign Exchange Reserves . . . .

Mutual Exchange . . . .

Stock Exchange . . . .

Stock Exchange Position . . . .

Stock Exchange Market . . . .

42. FACILITIES

Ample facilities . . . .

Adequate facilities . . . .

Basic facilities . . . .

Better facilities . . . .

Bank facilities

Banking facilities

Coaching facilities

Credit facilities

Equal facilities

Educational facilities

Extra ordinary facilities

Few facilities

Greater facilities

Hospital facilities

Irrigation facilities

Loan facilities

Legal facilities

Library facilities

Laboratory facilities

Lack of facilities

Medical facility

Modern facilities

Ordinary facility

Other facilities

Postal facilities

Physical facilities

Rail Road facilities

Railway facilities

Special facilities

Screening facilities

Transport facilities ....

Technical facilities ....

Training facilities ....

43. FACT

As a matter of fact ....

Apart from the fact / that ....

And the fact that the ....

And the fact is that ....

Acknowledge the fact that ....

By the fact that ....

But the fact ....

But the fact is that ....

Because of the fact that ....

Despite the fact that ....

Denying the fact that ....

Due to the fact / that ....

Fact of the case ....

From the fact that ....

Far from the fact that ....

For the fact that ....

Facts of the case ....

Facts of the matter ....

I know the fact that ....

I am aware of the fact that . . . .

I am conscious of the fact that . . . .

I am proud of the fact that . . . .

I must acknowledge the fact that . . . .

In fact . . . .

In the fact that . . . .

In point of fact . . . .

In view of the fact that . . . .

In spite of the fact that the . . . .

It is known fact . . . .

It is a fact that . . . .

It is the fact that . . . .

It is also the fact that . . . .

It is due to the fact that . . . .

Irrespective of the fact that . . . .

Not withstanding the fact that . . . .

Of the fact that . . . .

Recognise the fact that . . . .

Recognising the fact that . . . .

To the fact that . . . .

This is due to the fact that . . . .

44. <u>FORWARD</u>

Bring forward . . . .

Brought forward

Come forward

Comes forward

Came forward

Carry forward

Carried forward

Carrying forward

Goes forward

Going forward

Great step forward

Look forward

Leap forward

Looking forward

Move forward

Moving forward

March forward

Marching forward

Put forward

Step forward

Straight forward

To go forward

To bring forward

Will bring forward

We brought forward

45. FUNDAMENTAL

Fundamental Rule ....

Fundamental Role ....

Fundamental Rights ....

Fundamental Law ....

Fundamental Basis ....

Fundamental Principles ....

46. GAZETTED POSTS

Additional Secretary ....

Additional Commissioner ....

Assistant Secretary ....

Chief Secretary ....

Cabinet Secretary ....

Company Secretary ....

Chartered Accountant's ....

Chief Commissioner ....

Chief Election Commissioner ....

Claims Commissioner ....

Civil Supplies Commissioner ....

Deputy Secretary ....

Defence Secretary ....

Dy. Commissioner ....

Electrical Engineer ....

Executive Engineer ....

Food Secretary ....

Foreign Secretary ....

General Secretary ....

General Manager ....

Governor General ....

Governor General of India ....

Home Secretary ....

High Commissioner ....

Inspector General ....

Inspector General of Police ....

Income Tax Officer ....

Indian High Commissioner ....

Judicial Commissioner ....

Joint Secretary ....

Locomotive Superintendent ....

Labour Commissioner ....

Labour Secretary ....

Mechanical Engineer ....

Municipal Commissioner ....

Major General ....

Private Secretary ....

Post Master General ....

Superintending Engineer ....

Secretary General ....

Secretary of State ....

Superintendent of Police . . . .

Secy. of State for the Colonies . . . .

Secy. of State for the Home Deptt. . . . .

Secy. of State for War . . . .

Secretary Commissioner . . . .

Sanitary Commissioner . . . .

Special Secretary . . . .

Under Secretary . . . .

47. HAPPENED

As to what happened . . . .

That has happened . . . .

What happens . . . .

What happened . . . .

What has happened . . . .

What is happening . . . .

48. HOUSE

As the House knows . . . .

August House . . . .

As the Hon.Member . . . .

As the House . . . .

As the House is aware . . . .

Before the House . . . .

Before the House of Parliament ....

By the House ....

By this House ....

Before the House ....

Before this House ....

Both the Houses ....

By the other House ....

By the Hon. Member ....

Both the Houses of Parliament ....

Boarding & Lodging House ....

Coffee House ....

Cinema House ....

Entire House of Parliament ....

Entire House ....

Focus the attention of the House ....

For the House ....

From the other side of the House ....

For the House ....

From the other House ....

Hon'ble House ....

House is aware ....

House is aware that / the ....

House is aware of the fact that ....

House of People ....

House of Commons ....

House of Lords ....

House of Parliament

Houses of Parliament

Hon'ble Members of the House

Hon'ble Speaker

Hon'ble Members of the Opposition

In the House of People

I may tell the House

I have already told the House

Inform the House

I beg the House

I wish to assure the House

I would beg the House

I would ask the House

I would request the House

I have told the House

In the other House

In this House

In the House

Industrial Houses

In this hon'ble House

I may assure the House

Inside the House

I would like to assure the House

In the House of Commons

Leader of the House

Leader of the Opposition

Leader of the Party

Lower House

Member/s of Parliament

Members of the House

Monopoly House/s

Of the House

On this side of the House

On the other side of the House

Other side of the House

Outside the House

On this House

On the floor of the House

On the floor of this House

On the table of the House

Parliament House

Proceedings of the House

Power House

Slum House

Slaughter House

Speaker of the House

Since the House

Since the House knows

Since the House is aware

Two Houses of Parliament

This side of the House

This House is aware . . . .

To the House . . . .

Told the House . . . .

Upper House . . . .

When the House . . . .

49. I

I know there is . . . .

I know there is not . . . .

I know there has been . . . .

I know there have been . . . .

I know there will be . . . .

I see there is . . . .

I regret to say / that . . . .

I mean to say . . . .

I beg to support . . . .

I beg to state . . . .

I beg to submit . . . .

I beg to say . . . .

I beg to say that . . . .

I want to make . . . .

I want to see . . . .

I want to know . . . .

I believe that / the . . . .

I believe there are . . . .

I believe there will be . . . .

I rise to support / the . . . .

I rise to support the Bill . . . .

I rise to support the resolution . . . .

I take the liberty . . . .

I take this opportunity . . . .

I need not say . . . .

I need not say that . . . .

I need not say this . . . .

I need not state . . . .

I need not reply . . . .

I need not go . . . .

I need not go into the / matter . . . .

I need not tell that . . . .

I need not tell this . . . .

I need not tell you . . . .

I need not tell the House . . . .

I need not tell the Hon'ble Members . . . .

I think that is . . . .

I think there is . . . .

I think that you are . . . .

I think there will . . . .

I think you will . . . .

I think you will not . . . .

I think you will agree . . . .

I think you will agree with me . . . .

I think it is necessary ....

I can only / be / think ....

I can be / there ....

I can understand ....

I only wish ....

I only wish to say ....

I only understand ....

I only think ....

I only say / that ....

I only want / to say / to see ....

I have only to say / that ....

I want to refer ....

I want to make a reference ....

I venture / to say ....

I venture to say that ....

I venture to ask ....

I venture to ask that ....

I venture to report ....

I venture to suggest ....

I may venture ....

I may draw the attention of the ....

I draw the attention of the ....

I agree with him ....

I am instructing ....

I enclose herewith ....

50. I AM

I am sorry . . . .

I am very sorry . . . .

I am sorry to state . . . .

I am sorry to state that . . . .

I am sorry to tell you . . . .

I am sorry to know that . . . .

I am sorry to say that the . . . .

I am very sorry to say that the . . . .

I am grateful . . . .

I am very grateful . . . .

I am sure . . . .

I am quite sure . . . .

I am sure there is . . . .

I am glad . . . .

I am glad to know . . . .

I am glad to state . . . .

I am glad to state that . . . .

I am glad to see . . . .

I am glad to find . . . .

I am glad that the . . . .

I am glad to say that the . . . .

I am very glad . . . .

I am very glad to say that the . . . .

I am very pleased . . . .

I am happy ....

I am happy to announce ....

I am happy to say that the ....

I am very happy to say that the ....

I am going into the ....

I am not going into the ....

I am not going into the matter ....

I am not going into the case ....

I am confident ....

I am quite confident ....

I am rather confident ....

I am able to ....

I am able to think ....

I am unable to ....

I am unable to think ....

I am of the view ....

I am also of the view ....

I am only ....

I am only to say / that ....

I am only suggesting ....

I am trusting ....

I am trusting you ....

I am quite hopeful ....

I am quite certain ....

I am certain that you are ....

I am afraid ....

I am afraid that ....

I am anxious ....

I am anxious to know ....

I am very anxious ....

I am very anxious to know ....

I am of the opinion ....

I am not of the opinion ....

I am surprised/that ....

I am not surprised ....

I am instructed ....

I am instructed to state ....

I am instructed to inform you ....

I am aware of the ....

I am aware of the fact that the ....

I am directed to state ....

I am directed to inform you ....

I am in receipt of your letter ....

I am in receipt of your favour ....

I am in receipt of your esteemed favour ....

I am requested ....

I am requested to inform you ....

I am in a position ....

I am not in a position ....

I am of the view ....

I am told that ....

I am not saying/that ....

51. I DO / I DO NOT

I do not ....

I do not know ....

I do not see ....

I do not say ....

I do not wish ....

I do not wish to say ....

I do not want ....

I do not want to say ....

I do not want to say that ....

I do not want to request ....

I do not understand ....

I do not mean to say ....

I do not wish there is ....

I do not want to suggest ....

I do not think there is ....

52. I HAVE

I have been given to understand ....

I have no objection ....

I have no hesitation ....

I have pleasure ....

I have the pleasure ....

I have great pleasure ....

I have received . . . . .

I have received your letter . . . . .

I have said that . . . . .

I have referred . . . . .

I have heard . . . . .

I have carefully . . . . .

I have seen . . . . .

I have already stated / that . . . . .

I have already said / that . . . . .

I have already told you . . . . .

I have already pointed out . . . . .

I have already requested / you . . . . .

I have already emphasized . . . . .

I have already mentioned . . . . .

I have already explained . . . . .

I have already informed . . . . .

I have already informed you . . . . .

I have already informed the House . . . . .

I have already informed the Government . . . . .

I have already referred . . . . .

I have already conceded . . . . .

I have already instructed . . . . .

I have already considered . . . . .

I have already assured . . . . .

I have already assured the . . . .

I have no doubt . . . .

I have no reason . . . .

I have just now . . . .

I have just mentioned . . . .

I have just referred . . . .

I have to say a few words . . . .

I have the honour to say / that . . . .

I have the great honour . . . .

I have great affection . . . .

I have their / there . . . .

I have been there . . . .

I have brought forward . . . .

53. IMPORTANT

Foremost importance . . . .

It is important that . . . .

It is very important . . . .

It is most important . . . .

It is also important . . . .

Is the most important . . . .

More important . . . .

More important than . . . .

Most important . . . .

Most important than ....

Most important matters ....

Most important place ....

Most important thing ....

Most important sector ....

Much more important ....

Much more important than ....

Utmost importance ....

Very important ....

Very important place ....

Very great importance ....

Very important part ....

54. INDUSTRIES/INDUSTRIAL

Basic Industries ....

Cottage Industry/ies ....

Cotton Textile Industry ....

Cottage & Village Industries ....

Cottage & Small Scale Industries ....

Cottage & Handloom Industries ....

Commerce & Industry ....

Defence Industry ....

Film Industry ....

Heavy Industries ....

Industrial Capacity ....

Industrial Research ....

Industrial Nations ....

Industrial Workers ....

Industrial Relations ....

Industrial Development ....

Industrial Progress ....

Industrial Projects ....

Industrial Revolution ....

Industrial conditions ....

Industrial growth ....

Industrial Life ....

Industrial unit ....

Industrial & Agricultural ....

Industrial & Agricultural Projects ....

Industrial Disputes ....

Industrial Disputes Act ....

Industrial Finance Corporation ....

Industrial Development Corporation ....

Industrial Policy Resolution ....

Industrial Development Bank of India ....

Iron & Steel Industries ....

Large Scale Industries ....

Large number of Industries ....

Mining Industry/ies ....

Medium Industries ....

Oil Industry ....

Rate of Industrial growth ....

Steel Industry ....

Sugar Industry ....

Small Scale Industries ....

Textile Industry ....

Tourist Industry ....

Village Industries ....

55. INTEREST

In our interest/s ....

In our own interest/s ....

In the interest/s of the ....

In the interest/s of the country ....

In the interest/s of the Government ....

In the interest/s of the people ....

In the interest/s of the party ....

In the interest/s of the nation ....

Interest/s of the country ....

56. LEVEL

At all levels ....

At every level ....

At the present level ....

All India level . . . .

Certain level . . . .

Cabinet level . . . .

Central level . . . .

Centre & State level . . . .

District level . . . .

High level . . . .

Higher Level Committee . . . .

International level . . . .

Low level . . . .

Lower level . . . .

Level of living . . . .

Minimum level . . . .

Maximum level . . . .

National level . . . .

Personal level . . . .

Rural level . . . .

Regional level . . . .

State level . . . .

Village level . . . .

Various levels . . . .

Very high level . . . .

Very low level . . . .

57. MANNER

Arbitrary manner . . . .

And in like manner . . . .

Appropriate manner . . . .

Business like manner . . . .

From the manner . . . .

From the manner in which . . . .

Haphazard manner . . . .

Half hearted manner . . . .

In a manner . . . .

In any manner . . . .

In the manner of . . . .

In the manner in which . . . .

In such a manner . . . .

In such a manner in which . . . .

In the same manner . . . .

In the same manner in which . . . .

In such manners . . . .

In some manner . . . .

In this manner . . . .

In that manner . . . .

In every manner . . . .

In the best manner . . . .

In the right manner . . . .

In the wrong manner . . . .

In the right or wrong manner ....

Peaceful manner ....

Piecemeal manner ....

Rational manner ....

Realistic manner ....

Reasonable manner ....

Similar manner ....

Simple manner ....

Smooth manner ....

Systematic manner ....

Scientific manner ....

Satisfactory manner ....

To the manner in which ....

Thoughtful manner ....

Unsatisfactory manner ....

Wasteful manner ....

58. MATTER

All those matters ....

All these matters ....

About the matter ....

As the matter ....

All such matters ....

As the matter is important ....

As the matter is urgent ....

As a matter of fact ....

As a matter of course ....

As a matter of restraint ....

As a matter of right ....

As a matter of grace ....

As a matter of principle ....

As a matter of necessity ....

As a matter of convenience ....

As a matter of respect ....

As a matter of policy ....

As a matter of satisfaction ....

As a matter of favour ....

As a matter of pride ....

Early attention to the matter ....

Entire matter ....

Fundamental matters ....

Fact/s of the matter ....

Going into the matter ....

Going through the matters ....

I will consider the matter ....

I will arrange the matter ....

I shall arrange the matter ....

In the matter ....

In the matter of the ....

In such matters ....

In accordance with the matter ....

In this matter ....

In these matters ....

In all these matters ....

In all those matters ....

In regard to such matters ....

In regard to this matter ....

Into the matter ....

It is a matter of ....

It is a matter of concern ....

It is a matter of common concern ....

It is a matter of great concern ....

It is a matter of satisfactory ....

It is a matter of gratification ....

It is a matter of great pleasure ....

It is a matter of consideration ....

It is a matter of surprise ....

It is a matter of great respect ....

It is a matter of regret ....

It is a matter of great regret ....

It is a matter of congratulations ....

It is a matter of satisfaction ....

It is a matter of great satisfaction ....

It is a matter of importance ....

It is a matter of great importance ....

It is a matter of policy ....

It is a matter of pride . . . .

It is a matter of principle . . . .

It is a matter of favour . . . .

It is a matter of rejoicing . . . .

It is a matter of deep regret . . . .

It is a matter of thought . . . .

It is a matter of urgency . . . .

It is a matter of convenience . . . .

It is a matter of knowledge . . . .

It is a matter of common knowledge . . . .

It is a matter of common sense . . . .

It is a matter of common experience . . . .

Let us consider the matter . . . .

Over such matters . . . .

That is the matter . . . .

This is a matter . . . .

To go into the matter . . . .

To go through the matter . . . .

Very simple matter . . . .

Very important matter . . . .

Vital matter . . . .

What is the matter . . . .

What is the matter with you . . . .

We have arranged the matter . . . .

Who will arrange the matter . . . .

59. MEMBER

Hon'ble Member/s . . . .

Member of Parliament . . . .

Members of Parliament . . . .

Member in charge . . . .

Member of the Lok Sabha . . . .

Member of the Rajya Sabha . . . .

Member of the opposition . . . .

Members of the opposition . . . .

60. MEANS

By all means . . . .

By some means . . . .

By some means or other . . . .

By such means . . . .

By such other means . . . .

Do you mean to say . . . .

Within the means . . . .

Within their means . . . .

61. MENTIONED

Also mentioned . . . .

Above mentioned . . . .

As I mentioned . . . .

As has been mentioned . . . .

As it has been mentioned . . . .

Brief mentioned . . . .

Clearly mentioned . . . .

He mentioned . . . .

He has mentioned . . . .

He has not mentioned . . . .

Has been mentioned . . . .

Has also been mentioned . . . .

I mention . . . .

I have mentioned . . . .

I just mentioned . . . .

I have just mentioned . . . .

I have just now mentioned . . . .

I want to mention . . . .

I do not want to mention . . . .

I am mentioning . . . .

I am not mentioning . . . .

I may mention . . . .

I will mention . . . .

I would like to mention . . . .

I fail to mention . . . .

I failed to mention . . . .

I wish to mention . . . .

I also wish to mention . . . .

I shall mention . . . .

I will only mention . . . .

It is mentioned . . . .

It was mentioned . . . .

It has been mentioned . . . .

It has also been mentioned . . . .

It is also mentioned . . . .

It may also be mentioned . . . .

It should be mentioned . . . .

In which it is mentioned . . . .

In which it has been mentioned . . . .

Ought to have mentioned . . . .

Should have been mentioned . . . .

Special mention . . . .

There is no mention . . . .

Was mentioned . . . .

Were mentioned . . . .

Which were mentioned . . . .

Which has been mentioned . . . .

Will be mentioned . . . .

Worth mentioning . . . .

62. MIND

Bear in mind . . . .

Born in mind . . . .

Keep in mind . . . .

Kept in mind ....

Should be born in mind ....

63. MINISTER

Agriculture Minister ....

Council of Ministers ....

Cabinet Minister ....

Central Ministers ....

Chief Minister/s ....

Communication Minister/s ....

Commerce Minister ....

Commerce & Industry Minister ....

Dy. Minister ....

Dy..Prime Minister ....

Defence Minister ....

Education Minister ....

External Affairs Minister ....

Ex-Minister ....

Energy Minister ....

Food Minister ....

Former Minister ....

Hon'ble Prime Minister ....

Home Minister ....

Finance Minister

Hon'ble Finance Minister

Hon'ble Minister of Railways

Health Minister

Hon'ble Minister

I & B Minister

Irrigation Minister

Industry Minister

Irrigation & Power Minister

Leader of the Opposition

Lok Sabha

Lok Sabha & Rajya Sabha

Labour Minister

Law Minister

Minister of Labour & Employment

Minister of Food & Agriculture

Minister of Information & Broadcasting

Minister of Irrigation & Power

Minister of Parliamentary Affairs

Minister of External Affairs

Minister of Railways

Minister of Health

Minister of Rehabilitation

Minister of Transport

Minister of Industries

Minister of Law . . . .

Minister of State . . . .

Minister of Education . . . .

Minister of Commerce & Industry . . . .

Prime Minister . . . .

Planning Minister . . . .

Petroleum Minister . . . .

Parliamentary Affairs Minister . . . .

Rehabilitation Minister . . . .

Railway Minister . . . .

Rajya Sabha . . . .

Rajya Sabha & Lok Sabha . . . .

64. MINISTRY

Agriculture Ministry . . . .

Commerce & Industry Ministry . . . .

Commerce Ministry . . . .

Defence Ministry . . . .

Education Ministry . . . .

External Affairs Ministry . . . .

Finance Ministry . . . .

Foreign Ministry . . . .

Home Ministry . . . .

Irrigation & Power Ministry

Irrigation Ministry

Labour Ministry

Law Ministry

Ministry of Food & Agriculture

Ministry of Home Affairs

Ministry of Commerce & Industry

Ministry of Culture

Ministry of Communications

Ministry of Transport

Ministry of Transport and Communications

Ministry of Law, Justice and Company Affairs

Ministry of Labour & Employment

Ministry of Supply and Rehabilitation

Ministry of Steel & Mines

Ministry of Urban Development

Ministry of Irrigation & Power

Ministry of Human Resources

Ministry of Human Resources and Development

Ministry of Information and Broadcasting

Ministry of Chemicals & Fertilisers

Ministry of Shipping & Transport

Ministry of Works & Housing

Ministry of Tourism & Civil Aviation . . . .
Ministry of External Affairs . . . .
Ministry of Parliamentary Affairs . . . .
Ministry of Finance . . . .
Ministry of Agriculture . . . .
Ministry of Education . . . .
Ministry of Health . . . .
Ministry of Railways . . . .
Ministry of Labour . . . .
Ministry of Defence . . . .
Ministry of Rehabilitation . . . .
Ministry of Energy . . . .
Ministry of Welfare . . . .
Ministry of Petroleum . . . .
Rehabilitation Ministry . . . .
Welfare Ministry . . . .

65. NECESSARY

Are necessary . . . .
Absolutely necessary . . . .
All the more necessary . . . .
Became necessary . . . .
Become necessary . . . .
Because it is necessary . . . .
Deems necessary . . . .

Is it necessary

Is it not necessary

Is it absolutely necessary

I think it is necessary

If necessary

If it is necessary

If it were necessary

It is necessary

It is necessary to have

It is necessary to know

It is necessary to remember

It is necessary to emphasize

It is absolutely necessary

It is absolutely necessary that the

It is therefore necessary

It would be necessary

It would not be necessary

It will be necessary

It will not be necessary

It may be necessary

It may not be necessary

It was necessary

It is only necessary

It should not be necessary

It is very necessary

It is however necessary

It is equally necessary ....

It is hardly necessary ....

It will only be necessary ....

It will become necessary ....

It would become necessary ....

It seems to be necessary ....

More necessary ....

Necessary action ....

Necessary consequences ....

Very necessary ....

Was necessary ....

Whenever necessary ....

Will be necessary ....

Will also be necessary ....

Will become necessary ....

Were necessary ....

Wherever necessary ....

Will be necessary ....

Will not be necessary ....

Which is necessary ....

Which are necessary ....

Which was necessary ....

Which were necessary ....

What was necessary ....

Whether it is necessary ....

When it is necessary ....

Why it is necessary

Why is it necessary

66. OMISSION - TO

As to how

As to how many

As to how far

As to why

As to what

As to when

As to whether

As to where

As to whether or not

67. OPINION

Consensus of opinion

Difference of opinion

Differences of opinion

Expression of opinion

Express an opinion

Freedom of opinion

Humble opinion

In their opinion

In our opinion

In the opinion of . . . .

In his opinion . . . .

In his own opinion . . . .

In my opinion . . . .

I am of the opinion . . . .

My personal opinion . . . .

Personal opinion . . . .

Public opinion . . . .

Unanimity of opinion . . . .

We are clearly of the opinion . . . .

68. ORGANISATION

Labour Organisation . . . .

Local Organisation . . . .

Political Organisation . . . .

Private Organisation . . . .

State Organisation . . . .

States Re-organisation Commission . . . .

Voluntary Organisation . . . .

United Nations Organisation . . . .

69. OUGHT

Ought to be . . . .

Ought to be considered . . . .

Ought to have been . . . .

Ought to have known . . . .

70. OUT / OUTSET

At the outset . . . .

At the very outset . . . .

Bought out . . . .

Brought out . . . .

Come out . . . .

Get out . . . .

Made out . . . .

Out of/the . . . .

Out of place . . . .

Out of India . . . .

Out of order . . . .

Out of hand . . . .

Out of date . . . .

Out of doors . . . .

Out of position . . . .

Out of question . . . .

Out of this . . . .

Out of these . . . .

Out of the way . . . .

Outside India . . . .

Point out . . . .

Pointed out . . . .

Set out . . . .

Sort out . . . .

71. PARTY/IES

Akali Dal . . . .

B.J.P. . . . .

C.P.I. . . . .

C.P.I.(M) . . . .

Certain Other Parties . . . .

Communist Party . . . .

Communist Party of India . . . .

Congress Party . . . .

Congress President . . . .

Conservative Party . . . .

Democratic Party . . . .

General Secretary of the Congress . . . .

Indian National Congress . . . .

Janta Dal . . . .

Janta Party . . . .

Liberal Unionist Party . . . .

Liberal Party . . . .

Majority Party . . . .

Minority Party . . . .

Multi - Party . . . .

Multi - Party Rule ....

Multi - Party System ....

Muslim League ....

One - Party Rule ....

One - Party Leader ....

Opposition Parties ....

Party in Power ....

Political Party ....

Republic Party ....

Ruling Party ....

Single Party ....

Single Party Rule ....

Single Party System ....

Sociolist Party ....

Swatantra Party ....

Union Party ....

United Front ....

72. PART

Any part of the ....

Early part of the ....

Earlier part of the ....

Every part of India ....

Each & Every part of India ....

Good part of ....

Good part of the . . . .

Great part of . . . .

Greater part of / the . . . .

Greater part of the year . . . .

In the part of . . . .

In some parts . . . .

In the early part / of the . . . .

In any part of the country . . . .

In all parts of the world . . . .

In some parts of the world . . . .

In some parts of the country . . . .

In most parts of the country . . . .

In many parts of India . . . .

In many parts of the world . . . .

In different parts of the world . . . .

In different parts of the country . . . .

In other parts of the country . . . .

In the later part of . . . .

In our part of the world . . . .

In our part of the Country . . . .

In other parts of the world . . . .

Large part of . . . .

Large parts of the country . . . .

Large parts of the world . . . .

Major part of . . . .

Major part of the . . . .

Most significant part of / the

On the part of the

Other parts of India

On your part

Other parts of the country

Parts of India

Parts of the country

Parts of the world

Part of our

Part & Parcel

Real part of the

Real part of India

Remaining part of / the

Small parts of

Small part of / the

Some other parts of India

Vital part of the

73. PLACE

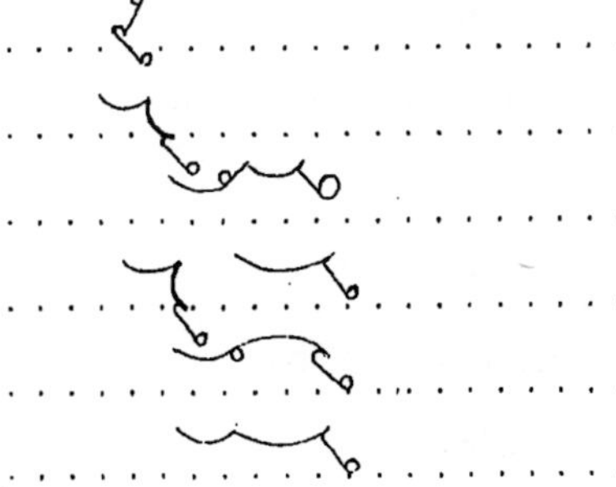

High place

In every place

In certain places

In other place

In some other place

In another place

In place of ....

In the next place ....

In such place ....

In the first place ....

In the second place ....

In the third place ....

In the last place ....

It has taken place ....

Most important place ....

No other place ....

Out of place ....

Some place ....

Some other place ....

That has taken place ....

74. POSITION

Bad position ....

Better position ....

Balance of payments position ....

Financial position ....

Foreign Exchange position ....

Good position ....

I am in a position ....

I am not in a position ....

In position ....

In a position

In this position

In a better position

In the same position

It is in a position

It is not in a position

Satisfactory position

They are in a position

They are not in a position

We are in a position

We are not in a position

Which are in a position

Which are not in a position

75. POSSIBLE

As far as possible

As early as possible

As soon as possible

As long as possible

As rapidly as possible

As quickly as possible

As might as possible

As much as possible

As much care as possible

As if it were possible

As it is possible

As well as possible

As near as possible

At your earliest possible

It is possible

It is not possible

It is possible that the

It is quite possible

It will be possible

It will not be possible

It would be possible

It may be possible

It may not be possible

It has been possible

It has not been possible

It is not yet possible

It is no longer possible

It would not be possible

It would have been possible

It would not have been possible

It should have been possible

It must be possible

Is it possible

Is it not possible

If possible

If it is possible

If it is not possible ....

Just possible ....

Just possible that ....

So far as possible ....

To the extent possible ....

That is possible ....

That is not possible ....

That has not been possible ....

This may be possible ....

This may not be possible ....

Utmost extent possible ....

Whether it is possible ....

Wherever possible ....

Whenever possible ....

Whatever possible ....

Whatever is possible ....

76. PURPOSE

For the purpose / of the ....

For the purposes ....

For this purpose ....

For that purpose ....

For what purpose ....

77. PURVIEW

Beyond of the purview of ....

From the purview of the ....

Out of the purview of ....

Outside the purview of ....

Under the purview of the ....

Within the purview of the ....

78. REPLY

Early reply ....

Early reply please ....

Favourable reply ....

I will reply ....

I would like to reply ....

In reply / to ....

In reply to the ....

In reply to my letter ....

In reply to this ....

In reply to that ....

In reply to a question ....

In your reply ....

In reply to your esteemed favour ....

In reply to your favour ....

In reply to your letter ....

In reply to your letter number

In reply to your letter dated

There is no reply

There is no reply to my letter

79. RELATIONS

Better & cordial relations

Better relations

Cordial relations

Commercial relations

Close relations

Close relationship

Cultural relations

Diplomatic relations

Feudal relations

Foreign relations

Friendly relations

Good relations

Harmonious relations

In relation to the

In relation to their

In their relations

In our relations

In relation to their

Intimate relations

Internal relations . . . .

International relations . . . .

Industrial relations . . . .

Labour relations . . . .

Near relations . . . .

Normal relations . . . .

Neighbourly relations . . . .

Near & Dear relations . . . .

Public relations . . . .

Trade relations . . . .

Very good relations . . . .

With relation to the . . . .

80. RECENT

In recent days . . . .

In recent weeks . . . .

In recent months . . . .

In recent years . . . .

In recent times . . . .

In recent past . . . .

81. RESPECT

In respect of . . . .

In this respect . . . .

In other respects . . . .

In some respect . . . .

In certain respects . . . .

In many respects . . . .

With respect to the . . . .

82. REGARD

As regards/the . . . .

Best regards . . . .

Convey my regards . . . .

Having regard to/the . . . .

Having regard to this matter . . . .

Having regard to these matters . . . .

Having regard to the fact that . . . .

In regard to/the . . . .

In regard to this . . . .

In regard to them . . . .

In this regard . . . .

In that regard . . . .

In regard to those . . . .

In regard to those matters . . . .

Kind regards . . . .

Pay my regards . . . .

With best regards . . . .

With regard to/the . . . .

With regard to this . . . .

With regard to that . . . .

With regard to those . . . .

With regard to those matters . . . .

With regard to those question . . . .

With regard to these things . . . .

With regard to such things . . . .

83. <u>REQUIREMENTS</u>

Actual requirements . . . .

According to the requirements . . . .

Basic requirements . . . .

Credit requirements . . . .

Country's requirements . . . .

Domestic requirements . . . .

Defence requirements . . . .

Development requirements . . . .

Essential requirements . . . .

Estimated requirements . . . .

Future requirements . . . .

Financial requirements . . . .

Genuine requirements . . . .

Internal requirements . . . .

Increased requirements . . . .

Long term requirements . . . .

Manpower requirements ....

Minimum requirements ....

Maximum requirements ....

Present requirements ....

Short term requirements ....

Special requirements ....

To meet the requirements ....

To meet our requirements ....

Your requirements ....

84. RESOURCES

Available resources ....

Adequate resources ....

Additional resources ....

Capital resources ....

Central resources ....

Enough resources ....

External resources ....

Financial resources ....

Further resources ....

Foreign resources ....

Foreign exchange resources ....

Human resources ....

Indian resources/India's resources ....

Lack of resources ....

Limited resources ....

Many resources ....

More resources ....

More and more resources ....

Mineral resources ....

Material resources ....

Mineral & Oil resources ....

Natural resources ....

Other resources ....

Overall resources ....

Power resources ....

Special resources ....

Unlimited resources ....

Water resources ....

Your resources ....

85. RESPONSIBILITY / IES

Collective responsibility ....

Duties and responsibilities ....

Higher responsibilities ....

Primary responsibility ....

Sense of responsibility ....

Serious responsibility ....

86. RELATED TO RAILWAYS

Break Down Plant ....

By Passenger Train ....

Central Railways ....

Defective Signal ....

District Traffic Manager ....

Eastern Railways ....

Electric Railways ....

First Class ....

First Class Passenger ....

Goods Traffic Committee ....

Indian Railways ....

Indian Railways Act ....

Locomotive Department ....

Locomotive & Engineering Committee ....

Locomotive Superintendent ....

Metro Railways ....

Metro Railways System ....

Metropolitan Railways ....

Northern Railways ....

Passenger Train ....

Passenger Traffic Committee ....

Railway Administration ....

Railway Electrification ....

Railway Board ....

Railway Directors . . . .

Railway Executive . . . .

Railway Manager . . . .

Railway Company . . . .

Railway Facilities . . . .

Railway Official . . . .

Railway Rates . . . .

Railway Fares . . . .

Railway Tickets . . . .

Railway Time . . . .

Railway Time Table . . . .

Railway Lines . . . .

Railway Engine . . . .

Railway Engine Driver . . . .

Railway Godown . . . .

Railway Goods . . . .

Railway Passengers . . . .

Railway Budget . . . .

Railway Budget Speech . . . .

Railway Budget Estimates . . . .

Railway Booking . . . .

Railway Booking Office . . . .

Railway Booking Staff . . . .

Railway Employees . . . .

Railway Federations . . . .

Railway Staff . . . .

Railway Trade Union ....

Railway Station ....

Railway Strike ....

Railway Ticket Collector ....

Railway Traffic ....

Railway Board Act ....

Railway Minister / Ministry ....

Second Class ....

Second Class Passenger ....

Second Class Ticket ....

Second Class Compartment ....

South Eastern Railways ....

Southern Railways ....

Station Master ....

Third Class Compartment ....

Traffic Manager ....

Under- Ground Railways ....

Western Railways ....

87. RELATED TO COURTS/LEGAL

Civil Courts ....

Criminal Courts ....

Court of Appeal ....

Court of Criminal Appeal ....

Central Criminal Court ....

Counsel for the Defence . . . .
Counsel for the defendant . . . .
Counsel for the plaintiff . . . .
Counsel for the prisoner . . . .
Counsel for the prosecution . . . .
Chief Justice of India . . . .
District Courts . . . .
Divisional Court . . . .
District & Session Judge . . . .
Executive power . . . .
Federal Court . . . .
High Court . . . .
High Court Judge/s . . . .
High Court Judgement . . . .
Judicial power . . . .
Judgment summons . . . .
Justice of the peace . . . .
Lord Chancellor . . . .
Lord Chief Justice . . . .
Lower Court . . . .
Lower Court's Judgement . . . .
Lower Court's Statement . . . .
Legislative power . . . .
Law & Order Situation . . . .
Ordinary Court . . . .
Queen's Bench . . . .

Queen's Division . . . .

Supreme Court . . . .

Supreme Court Judge . . . .

Supreme Court of India . . . .

88. REQUIRED

Are required . . . .

Are required to be . . . .

Do you required . . . .

If he required . . . .

It will be required . . . .

It will not be required . . . .

It may be required . . . .

It may not be required . . . .

It requires . . . .

This requires . . . .

Wherever required . . . .

Which will require . . . .

Which is required . . . .

Who are required . . . .

Was required . . . .

Were required . . . .

Which may require . . . .

Which may be required . . . .

Will be required . . . .

Would be required ....

Would not be required ....

We require ....

We are required ....

We are required to ....

89. SALUTATIONS / ENDINGS

Ladies & Gentlemen ....

Mr. Speaker/Sir ....

Mr. Dy. Speaker/Sir ....

Mr. Chairman/Sir ....

Mr. Dy. Chairman/Sir ....

Mr. Vice-Chancellor/Sir ....

Mr. Vice-Chairman/Sir ....

My Dear ....

My Dear Sir ....

My Dear Madam ....

My Dear Friend ....

My Hon'ble Friend ....

My Dear Fellow Citizens ....

My Dear Brother ....

My Dear Sister ....

My Dear colleagues ....

My Hon'ble colleagues ....

Sincerely yours ....

Very truly yours ....

Very sincerely ....

Very sincerely yours ....

Vice-Chairman/Sir ....

Your favour ....

Your esteemed favour ....

Yours respectfully ....

Yours faithfully ....

Yours sincerely ....

Yours truely ....

Yours obediently ....

Yours affectionately ....

90. SHALL/SHOULD

He should not ....

He should be ....

He should be there ....

I should ....

I should be ....

I should not ....

I should have ....

I should be glad ....

I should be grateful ....

I should like ....

I should like to say ....

I should like to say that the	
I should like to say a few words	
I should like to know	
I should like to know that	
I should like to this House	
I should like to request	
I beg to submit	
I beg to request	
I beg to suggest	
I beg to acknowledge receipt of your favour	
I beg to acknowledge receipt of your letter	
I beg to call attention	
I shall arrange	
I shall arrange the matter	
I shall submit	
I shall now submit	
I shall be grateful	
I shall be very grateful	
I shall be glad/to know	
I shall be glad to state/that	
I shall be glad to say/that	
I shall be glad to have	
I Shall be there	
I shall be there	
I shall not be there	

I shall go into the

I shall go into the matter

I should like to draw the attention

I should like to draw your attention

I should like to draw the attention of the Hon.Member

I should like to draw the attention of the House

I should like to submit

I should like to point out

I should like to acknowledge the

I should like to acknowledge the letter

I should like to acknowledge your letter

I should like to state/that

It should also be

It should be referred

It should be able to

It should not be able to

Should be

Should be taken

Should not be taken

Should not be done

Should have been

Should have been there

Should not have been

Should be considered

Should not be there

Should be there
Should be born in mind
There should have been
There should be
There should not be
They should have been
That he should
We shall be able to
What should be the
Which should be
We should not
We shall be obliged
We shall expect
We shall be grateful
We shall be very grateful
We shall be glad/ to have/ to know
We shall be glad to hear/to receive
We should be glad to have
We should have/the
We should like to have
We should go into / the matter
We should not
We should not go
We should not think/that
We should not think only
We should take the

We should take them . . . .

We should take up the . . . .

We should know . . . .

We should know it . . . .

We should know that . . . .

We should try . . . .

We should be proud . . . .

We should be proud of the fact that . . . .

We should go . . . .

We should go forward . . . .

We should go out . . . .

We should also . . . .

We should also try . . . .

We should view . . . .

We should welcome . . . .

We should come out . . . .

We should go . . . .

We should go forward . . . .

We should go out . . . .

We should like . . . .

We should like to know . . . .

We should be . . . .

We should be able to . . . .

We should have been . . . .

You should be . . . .

You should be there . . . .

You should not be there

You should not have been

You should not have been there

91. SORT

All sorts of

All sorts of the

All sorts of things

All sorts of conditions

All sorts of difficulties

By all sorts of

Such sort of

Such sort of things

What sort of

92. STAGE

At this stage

At the initial stages

In the initial stages

93. STATEMENT

As our statement

Audited statement

Audited statement of accounts ....

Auditors statement ....

Categorical statement ....

Enclosed statement ....

From the statement ....

In this statement ....

In his statement ....

In her statement ....

In our statement ....

In their statement ....

Of this statement ....

Of his statement ....

Of such statement ....

Statement of accounts ....

Statement of objects ....

Statement of objects & reasons ....

Welcome statement ....

94. SYSTEM

Alternative system ....

Banking system ....

Bad system ....

Better system ....

Budgetary system ....

Democratic system	....
Distribution system	....
Economic system	....
Educational system	....
Federal system	....
Federal system of Government	....
Good system	....
Irrigation system	....
Judicial system	....
Legal system	....
Multy party system	....
Much better system	....
Present system	....
Present system of Government	....
Proposed system	....
Parliamentary system	....
Political system	....
Public Distribution System	....
Rational system	....
Road system	....
Social system	....
Socio-economic system	....
This system	....
Transport system	....

Tax system ....

Up to the present system ....

95. TIME

At times ....

At this time ....

At a time ....

At the time ....

At one time ....

At that time ....

At all times ....

At all times to come ....

At any time ....

At some time ....

At the same time ....

At the present time ....

At any period of time ....

At your earliest possible time ....

After some time ....

After a long time ....

Appropriate time ....

Considerable time ....

Considerable time to come ....

Few weeks time ....

Few months time ....

For a time ....

For a short time ....

For all time ....

For several time ....

For some time ....

For some time past ....

For the first time ....

For the second time ....

For the third time ....

For a long time ....

For a very long time ....

For such a long time ....

For want of time ....

For the time being ....

From time to time ....

From time immemorial ....

High time ....

In a short time ....

In the short time ....

In the short period of time ....

In the meantime ....

In a month's time ....

In a course of time ....

In recent time ....

It is time ....

It is not appropriate time ....

Last time . . . .

Long time past . . . .

Peace time . . . .

Point of time . . . .

Requisite time . . . .

Reasonable time . . . .

Short span of time . . . .

Stipulated time . . . .

Some time past . . . .

Some time ago . . . .

Some time back . . . .

So many times . . . .

This time . . . .

Till some time . . . .

Till such time . . . .

Till some time past . . . .

Time Table . . . .

Time to time . . . .

Time & again . . . .

Time & attention . . . .

Time & place . . . .

Upto the present time . . . .

War time . . . .

Waste of time . . . .

Within the short time . . . .

96. UNDERTAKING

Central Undertakings ....

Electricity Undertakings ....

Industrial Undertakings ....

Public Undertakings ....

Private Undertakings ....

Public Sector Undertakings ....

Private Sector Undertakings ....

State Undertakings ....

Public & Private Sector Undertakings ....

97. UP / UPTO

Upto date ....

Upto date information ....

Ups & downs ....

Uptill now ....

Upto the mark ....

Upto the present ....

Upto the present time ....

Upto present time ....

Upto a certain point ....

Upto a certain extent ....

Upto the last moment ....

98. VIEW

Another point of view . . . .

Coming into view . . . .

Correct view . . . .

Different point of view . . . .

From your view . . . .

From their view . . . .

From the point of view . . . .

From our point of view . . . .

General view . . . .

General view point . . . .

General point of view . . . .

In my view . . . .

In view of the . . . .

In view of this . . . .

In view of that . . . .

In view of these things . . . .

Large view . . . .

Larger view . . . .

Longer view . . . .

Liberal view . . . .

My view . . . .

My own view . . . .

My own view of the matter . . . .

My personal view . . . .

Optimistic view ....

Point of view ....

Pessimistic view ....

Perochial view ....

Same view ....

This point of view ....

To keep in view ....

View point ....

Very serious view ....

With a view to ....

What is your view ....

Your point of view ....

99. WITH

With retrospective effect ....

With effect from ....

With immediate effect ....

With reference to / the ....

With reference to which ....

With regards ....

With regard to / the ....

With due regards ....

With due respect ....

With regard to the fact that ....

With great regard ....

With each other

With a view to

With the request

With the request that

With the rest of the country

With great pleasure

With great respect

With relation to / the

With the people

With respect to

With best wishes

100. WILL

I will not

I will not be

I will not be in a position

I will be there / I will not be there

I will be suggested

I will be proposed

I will not be proposed

I will be remembered / that

I will only say

I will not say

I will only say that

I will tell you

I will urge you ....

I will urge the ....

I will urge the Government ....

I will urge the Hon.Members ....

I will urge the Hon.Minister ....

I will arrange ....

I will arrange the matter ....

I will request ....

I will request that ....

I will only request ....

I will briefly ....

I will forward ....

I will therefore ....

I will consider the matter ....

I will request the Hon.Members ....

I will request the Hon.Minister ....

It will not be ....

It will not be in a position ....

If he will ....

They will not ....

They will only be ....

They will be made ....

There will not be ....

This will ....

We will be there ....

We will not be there . . . .

We will be able to . . . .

We will not be able to . . . .

Will be taken . . . .

Will have to be taken . . . .

Will not be taken . . . .

Will not be given . . . .

Will not be there . . . .

Will be considered . . . .

Will agree that . . . .

Will be able to . . . .

Will be glad to say . . . .

Will be glad to say that . . . .

Will be glad to know . . . .

Will be glad to see . . . .

Will be glad to hear . . . .

Will be glad to state . . . .

Will be glad to state that . . . .

Will be glad to note . . . .

Will be glad to have . . . .

Will be called upon . . . .

Will be required . . . .

Will be met . . . .

Will be arranged . . . .

Will only say . . . .

Will only say that . . . .

Will only be able to ....

Will you kindly ....

Will you allow ....

Will you pleased ....

Will you please refer ....

Will you please refer to your letter ....

What will be the ....

Which will not be ....

You will find ....

You will remember ....

101. WOULD

He would ask that the ....

I would ....

I would like ....

I would not like ....

I would be ....

I would not ....

I would not be ....

I would have ....

I would not have ....

I would like to refer ....

I would like to suggest ....

I would like to request ....

I would like to add that ....

I would like to spell out . . . .

I would like to demand . . . .

I would like to conclude . . . .

I would like to answer . . . .

I would like to submit that . . . .

I would like to say that the . . . .

I would like the Ministers . . . .

I would like you . . . .

I would like you very much . . . .

I would like to draw the attention of the . . . .

I would like to assure you . . . .

I would like to say a few words . . . .

I would like to take . . . .

I would like to take this opportunity . . . .

I would like to ask the . . . .

I would also like to ask / that . . . .

I would also like to see . . . .

I would like to emphasise . . . .

I would also like to know . . . .

I would also like to say that . . . .

I would also like to state / that . . . .

I would also like to point out . . . .

I would ask . . . .

I would say that . . . .

I would suggest . . . .

I would suggest that . . . .

I would therefore

It would be

It would be right

It would be wrong

It would mean

It would be better

I would quote

They would be

They would not be

They would be able to

We would not have been

What would happen

I would / be / have

I would remember the

I would ask them

I would ask the Hon.Members

I would ask the Hon.Minister

I would request

I would request the Hon.Members

I would request the Hon.Minister

I would not say that

I would plead

I would plead that

I would pray

I would point out

I would be grateful

I would also ask/that

I would seek

I would say a few words

I would emphasise

I would be happy

I would be happy to say tha

I would be happy to kno

I would be happy to state

I would like this

I would like to state/that

I would like to mention

I would like to seek

I would like to ask/that

I would like to know

I would like to suggest
to the Hon.Member

I would like to suggest
to the Hon.Minister

I would like to sound

I would like to support

I would like to submit

I would like to ask the Hon.Members

I would like to ask the Hon.Minister

I would like to ask the House

I would like to assure him

I would like to assure you

I would like to assure the Hon.Member/s

I would like to assure the Hon.Minister/s . . . .

I would like to assure the House . . . .

I would like to remind . . . .

I would like to remind the House . . . .

I would like to deal with . . . .

I would like to start . . . .

I would like to congratulate . . . .

I would like to begin . . . .

I would like to apologise . . . .

I would like to express . . . .

I would like to complement . . . .

I would like to reiterate . . . .

I would like to stress . . . .

I would like to point out . . . .

I would like to tell/you . . . .

I would like to tell the House . . . .

I would like to place . . . .

I would like to make . . . .

I would like to draw the . . . .

I would like to draw the attention of the House . . . .

I would like to draw the attention of the Hon.Members . . . .

I would like to draw the attention of the Hon.Minister . . . .

I would like to have

I would like to have the opportunity

We would be

We would not be

We would also be

We would like to know

We would like it

We would also like

We would also like to know

We would also like to have

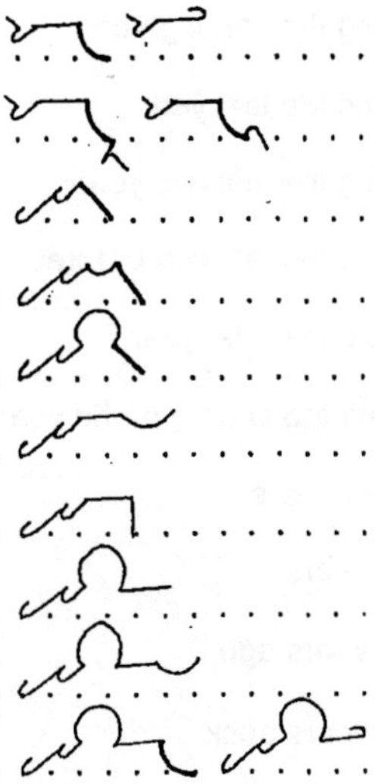

102. YEAR

At the beginning of the year

At the end of the year

All the year round

Assessment year

By the year end

Current year

Couple of years

During the year

During the current year

During the next few years

During the year under review

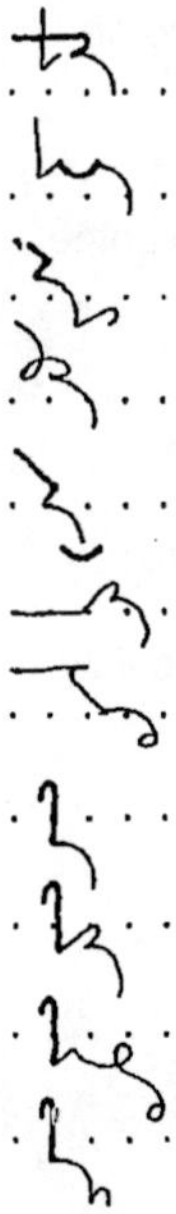

During the coming year
During the last year
During the last two years
During the last two or three years
During the past year
During the course of the year
Earlier years
Few years
Few years ago
Few years back
From year to year
For the year
For some years
For some years to come
For several years
For several years to come
For the current year
First Five Year Plan
For the last two years
For the year under review
Half year
Hundreds of years
In a couple of years
In recent years
In the year
In the coming year

In the current year ....

In the last two years ....

In the last two or three years ....

In the last few years ....

In the course of the year ....

In the course of the last year ....

Lean year ....

Leap year ....

Many years ....

Many years ago ....

Many years to come ....

Next year ....

Next few years ....

Of the year under review ....

Over the years ....

Past few years ....

Some years ago ....

Some years back ....

Some years to come ....

Since the year ....

Successive year ....

Subsequent years / to come ....

Second Five Year Plan ....

Through-out the year ....

Two or three years ....

Two and a half years ....

Two and a half years ago ....

Year by year ....

Year to year ....

Years ago ....

Years & years ago ....

103. SOME OTHER PHRASES

As far as I can ....

As far as I know ....

As far as ....

As a whole ....

As you know ....

As if it were ....

As much as were ....

As has been ....

Above their ....

At the end of the ....

At the present moment ....

As we may ....

As well as usual ....

As well as can be ....

As well as ....

As soon as we can ....

As soon as they ....

Arms and Ammunitions ....

Anti Social Elements ....

Around the words ....

As much as were ....

As if it were ....

It can only be ....

It may only be ....

On the whole ....

We have received ....

So far as ....

So far as the ....

On the one hand ....

On the other hand ....

Backward classes ....

Scheduled classes ....

Scheduled Castes ....

Scheduled Tribes ....

SCs & STs ....

Until & unless ....

Unless & until ....

Stresses & strains ....

Yes or no ....

Yesterday afternoon ....

Yesterday evening ....

Yesterday morning ....

Last week ....

Next week ....

Next month . . . .
This month . . . .
Most of us . . . .
Balance of payments . . . .
Balance of payments position . . . .
There is no other . . . .
There is no justification . . . .
There is no other way . . . .
There is no provision . . . .
Has to be there . . . .
Has been there . . . .
Which has to be . . . .
We have their . . . .
We have been there . . . .
If he were . . . .
If there is to be . . . .
If it is the . . . .
It is be there . . . .
Upon their . . . .
Over there or their . . . .
Though there is . . . .
Before there is . . . .
If there is . . . .
In their case . . . .
In which there is . . . .
Whenever there is . . . .

Though there is

More than their

Take their way

Pending their decision

With reference to the

In compliance with the

In consultation with the

From the other

Or the other

Somehow of the other

In favour of the

In the context of the

In the first instance

In the light of the

In charge of the

In consequence of

In a few days

In reference to

It is hoped that

It is essential that

It is important to remember that

It is obvious that the

It has been reported

It gives me a great pleasure

We have to consider

Which have to be

Interim dividend ....

Interim Bonus ....

On the subject ....

On several occasions ....

Paid up capital ....

Per capita income ....

Much better of ....

Much better than ....

Much better position ....

In accordance with ....

In accordance with the ....

In reference to which ....

With reference to which ....

With relation to ....

Have been expected ....

Have been informed ....

Have been returned ....

We are grateful ....

We are very grateful ....

National Insurance Account ....

Co-operative Societies ....

Socialistic Pattern of Society ....

Stock Exchange ....

Reserve Bank of India ....

Public & Private Sectors ....

Research and Development ....

Water & Electricity Deptt. ....

Government Sectors ....

Cross purposes ....

Media and Instruction ....

In response to the ....

There must have been ....

On this occasion ....

It can only be ....

It may only be ....

If it is not ....

Is it be not ....

If it were ....

In which it is ....

In which it has appeared ....

Able to make ....

Able to thank ....

At any rate ....

And the contrary ....

End of the month ....

It seems to us ....

If you will favour me ....

While there is ....

Please let us know ....

On the subject ....

Next week ....

Carried out ....

Very successful

Three weeks time

Further than the

Under separate cover

Yesterday attention

Please let me know

Let us hope

Scheduled areas

Non-schedule

Non-schedule areas

Scheduled time

Scheduled Banks

Already there

As if there is

As if there is no

Against there

If there is

If there is not

If there had been

If there is no objection

If there is any objection

In their case

In their way

In their own way

In their position

In which there are

Before there is

Has to be there

Has been there

How can there be

He may not be there

Even there is

More than their

Making their/way

May be there

May not be there

Take their place

Take their seats

Take their time

To make their

To make their way

To make up their

Unless there is

Unless there has been

While there is

Notes:

Other Books on

GENERAL SERIES

1. Chanakya Neeti **(New)**
2. Helpline for Stressed Parents **(New)**
3. Grow Rich with Peace of Mind **(New)**
4. How to be Fit and Young **(New)**
5. How to Succeed in Life **(New)**
6. 100 Ways to Develop Self Confidence
7. Child Development
8. Abraham Lincoln A Complete Biography
9. Mein Kampf My Struggle
10. Think and Grow Rich
11. The Art of Personality Development
12. Positive Mind Power
13. Travel & Tourism An Industry Facilitator
14. World's Great Authors And Poets
15. Effective Editing Help Yourself in Becoming a Good Editor
16. Smart House-Keeping for Modern Women
17. Develop Super Power Memory
18. World's Great Personalities
19. Personality Plus
20. Power of Positive Thinking
21. Art of Successful Parenting
22. A Handbook of Etiquettes
23. World's Great Scientists
24. Body Language
25. Art of Successful Living

26. Jokes for All
27. Selected Dohas
28. Baby Names for Girls **(New)**
29. Baby Names for Boys **(New)**
30. Art of Public Speaking
31. The World's Greatest Speeches
32. Group Discussions
33. Personality Development
34. Think Positive & Things Will Go Right
35. Once in a Blue Moon (A Tantra Tale)
36. God is Dead
37. Travel India (A Complete Guide for Tourists)
38. Glimpses of Urdu Poetry
39. How to Reduce Tension
40. A Book of Stenography **(New)**
41. Baby Names for the Boy
42. Baby Names for the Girl
43. Ripples in Tranquil Waters

Unit No. 220, 2nd Floor, 4735/22, Prakash Deep Building,
Ansari Road, Darya Ganj, New Delhi- 110002
Ph.: 23280047, 9811594448
E-mail : lotuspress1984@gmail.com, www.lotuspress.co.in